Bob Ward

Kickstart
Your Creativity

Think left and think right and think low and think high.
Oh, the thinks you can think up if only you try!

DR SEUSS, 'OH, THE THINKS YOU CAN THINK!'

Kickstart Your Creativity

The IDEAS BOOK

Mike Hutcheson & Rebecca Webster

Hodder Moa Beckett

National Library of New Zealand Cataloguing-in-Publication Data
Hutcheson, Mike.
Kickstart your creativity: the ideas book / Mike Hutcheson & Rebecca Webster. 1st ed.
ISBN 1-86958-968-8
1. Creative ability. 2. Problem solving. I. Webster, Rebecca, 1967–
II. Title.
153.35—dc 21

Text © Rebecca Webster & Mike Hutcheson 2003
Illustrations © Mike Hutcheson 2003
The moral rights of the authors have been asserted
Design and format © Hodder Moa Beckett Publishers Ltd 2003

Published in 2003 by Hodder Moa Beckett Publishers Ltd
[a member of the Hodder Headline Group]
4 Whetu Place, Mairangi Bay
Auckland, New Zealand

Cover design by Grace Design
Produced by BookNZ
Printed in China by Everbest Printing Co., Ltd.

All rights reserved. No part of this publication may be reproduced or transmitted in any form or by any means, electronic or mechanical, including photocopying, recording, or any information storage and retrieval system, without permission in writing from the publisher.

Contents

Suppose someone were to look for something that had no shape; to pursue something that didn't move; to find something that wasn't in any real place; to dig for something that wasn't under anything; to look for something that had no appearance. That someone might be searching for ideas.

D. PERKINS, 'THE MIND'S BEST WORK'

Acknowledgements 7	Pay homage 43
Foreword 9	Play with the palette 45
Introduction 11	Go west 47
How to use this book 19	Make connections 49
	Contrast 51
Go off the rails .21	Consider consequences 53
Improve 23	Catch your thoughts 55
Adapt and modify 25	Start hoarding .57
Make analogies .27	Combine 59
Rummage nature 29	Drawings, diagrams and doodles 61
Know hearts and minds 31	Distort and mutate 63
Picture the person 33	Divvy up 65
Break rules and push boundaries 35	Extract the essence 67
Bounce off others 37	Turn up the heat 69
Fly in the face of failure 39	Experience 71
Call on cliché 41	Dare to be naïve 73

Falsify	75
Blame it on Bob	77
Make the familiar strange	79
Love it or shove it	81
Swap hats	83
Do the opposite — flip, reverse, rotate	85
Adjust the focus	87
Globalise	89
Tap humour	91
Swelligantify	93
Invent from irritation	95
Go literal	97
Look in the 'wrong' place	99
Metamorph	101
Don't overlook the obvious	103
Change the pace	105
Explore paradox	107
Personify	109
Change identity	111
Step into an animal's world	113
Think like a kid	115
Swap eyes	117
What's hot and what's not?	119
Good questions create the best answers	121
Do you really need a bigger boat?	123
Recycle	125
Waste not want not	127
Start with the ridiculous	129
Examine the explanation	131
Reframe	133
Do a double take	135
Shape and form	137
Savour your spilt milk	139
Swing to the music	141
Simplify	143
Beef up or trim down	145
Be solution-focused	147
Explore myths, legends and fairytales	149
Tinker with style	151
Substance and structure	153
Find a ring-in	155
What's that smell?	157
Symbolise	159
Hindsight and foresight	161
Translate	163
Hitch a ride	165
Switch address	167
Visualise	169
Find other uses	171
Wordplay	173
Zoom in or fade out	175
Break bread	177
Exercise	179
Search the web	181
Explore parody	183
Pull from politics and protest	185
Sleep on it	187
Bibliography	189

Acknowledgements

To acknowledge individuals would be almost unfair as this book has emerged from observing the styles and tribulations of about 200 talented and dedicated staff at Saatchi & Saatchi over a period of four or five years. For their candour, co-operation, enthusiasm and friendship we humbly salute them.

Then there are the other disciples of creativity who have written their own thoughts on the subject and whose works we have scoured seeking to pull together the threads that might be relevant to a New Zealand audience. A full bibliography is contained at the back of the book for those who wish to do further reading.

New Zealand has produced many original thinkers — our per capita rate of patent applications is second in the world — and we hope this book will help inspire a few more.

Our thanks also to Kevin Chapman and Jane Hingston of Hodder Moa Beckett who recognised the need for such a book and who have encouraged and guided us through the editorial process.

Finally, to Will and Jan and our respective children who have put up with us being AWOL from family duties due to 4.30 am starts and 2.00 am finishes while the book came together. And to our friends and colleagues, who have lent their comments and support, we thank you for your time, love and patience.

Mike Hutcheson & Rebecca Webster
August 2003

Foreword

Saatchi & Saatchi's dream is to become the hottest ideas shop on the planet. Key to this is identifying, hiring and nurturing ideas people. This book helps in the nurturing phase. It gives dozens of ways to unblock a clogged brain when faced with the daunting task of thinking up something new.

It was originally conceived five years ago when Rebecca was working in our offices in Wellington and Auckland. Having come from a highly structured and bureaucratic environment in the Public Health system, she found the creative atmosphere of Saatchi & Saatchi to be fascinating and refreshing. Instead of addressing issues according to a fixed protocol and achieving predictable outcomes, Rebecca found a whole company of individuals who didn't seem to follow a rulebook yet consistently created inspirational advertising.

After many sleepless nights she finally found method in their madness. She detected a number of techniques with which they addressed problems. Rather than being chaotic she found them to be incredibly hardworking (or at least that's what she told me!) and disciplined in their apparent chaos.

Rebecca and Hutch (who ran our Auckland office and was therefore able to bring to bear his experience) then honed and polished these techniques into a collection. Including cartoons, quotes and anecdotes, their book also gives examples of how such creative 'triggers' have worked not only for our people but also for inventors, writers, artists and entrepreneurs through the ages.

Fascinated and stimulated by the manner in which intuitive people approach problems, they have trawled through more literature on the subject than you need to know about to share with us the stimuli (and the tricks) people use in order to bring new ideas to life.

Apparent lack of method disguises the fact that rather than single-mindedly pursuing one sequential route to a solution creative people have the ability to simultaneously pursue many. They will swarm over problems, attacking them from many sides at once until they find unique ways in. Solutions often so elegant in their simplicity, others ask: 'Why didn't I think of that?'

Kevin Roberts
CEO Saatchi & Saatchi Worldwide

Introduction

The air is full of ideas. They are knocking you in the head all the time. You only have to know what you want, then forget it, and go about your business. Suddenly, the idea will come through. It was there all the time.

HENRY FORD

What is creativity?

One of the best definitions of creativity we have come across is from Albert Szent-Georgi, the discoverer of vitamin C, who said, 'Creativity is seeing what everyone else has seen and thinking what no one else has thought.' Another definition says creativity is 'Making the familiar strange and the strange familiar.'

So is there a process for making this happen? We don't believe so. We think 'creative process' is an oxymoron. On the other hand a notion that has always fascinated us is creating conditions or environments in which creativity is able to flourish, producing outcomes that are commercially, socially or culturally relevant.

The path to fame and fortune is littered with the bones of people who died trying to find someone to accept their ideas. Conversely, many innovative ideas, new products or concepts are launched to a public that doesn't seem to want them. In all cases, better understanding of the diversity of how people think could have saved a lot of time, money and pain.

We each think differently and approach problems in our own unique ways. It is therefore important to understand the mentality of others so we may better comprehend and share ideas. There are many proprietary tools that can help us do that. Broadly speaking, our problem-solving and innovation styles will be based on a combination of our intelligence and personality.

We all have different personalities

Pioneer psychiatrist Carl Jung developed the theory that individuals have a psychological type. He believed that we use four functions in our lives: we perceive information either through our senses or intuition, then decide based on either objective logic or subjective feelings. Jung also identified an order of preference for these functions. That used most frequently becomes the 'dominant' function, supported by auxiliary, tertiary, and inferior functions.

He also asserted that individuals are either 'extroverted' or 'introverted' in their dominant function. He felt that the dominant function was so important that it overshadowed all other functions in terms of defining personality type. In this context 'extro' is a prefix meaning 'without' and 'intro' is a prefix meaning 'within'. If we are most comfortable looking towards the outer world of activity or words, we are called extroverted; if towards the inner world of ideas, information or thoughts, we are called introverted. Unfortunately, through popular use, the words introversion and extroversion have become synonymous with shyness and outgoing-ness — misleading definitions in terms of how we process information.

Thus, broadly speaking, we end up with 'sensible' (sensing) and 'intuitive' people who may be either 'introverted' or 'extroverted', giving a number of categories or groups into which an individual might slot.

Some of us choose to rely on our senses, things we see, hear, touch, smell and feel.

Some prefer taking in information through a sixth (intuitive) sense. Sensing people are detail-oriented; they want facts and trust them. The quintessential intuitive, on the other hand, was Albert Einstein whose unconventional thinking revolutionised science. He could see patterns where others saw chaos and believed that 'imagination is more important than knowledge'.

Each day we spontaneously do or say things, as well as withdrawing into an inner world of thoughts. If a working day has been hectic and full of interaction, an extrovert may feel the need to be left alone to contemplate. Conversely, an introvert who has been working in isolation all day, may feel the need to party on down at night.

Of course psychological typology did not originate with Carl Jung. As long ago as the fifth century BC, the physician Hippocrates classified four temperaments: melancholic, sanguine, phlegmatic and choleric. So mankind has been aware of differing minds for a long time. The topic of personality types is too broad for us to do more than mention it in passing in this introduction, but there is a wealth of literature on the subject if you wish to do further reading and many online tests are available. Although, for validity, we would urge any testing be conducted by professionals, Internet websites offering tests such as Myers-Briggs, based on Jungian psychology, can be used for a better understanding of your own type.

We all have different types of intelligence

The other major influence on our ability to generate ideas is our intelligence. We are not referring to IQ scale, in terms of high or low, but to types of intelligence. Educators have long been aware of differing learning styles and now widely recognise the importance of Howard Gardner's Theory of Multiple Intelligences.

This theory, first published in the early 1980s, has caught the imagination of teachers and the general public alike. Basically, Gardner (Professor at Harvard Graduate School of Education, Adjunct Professor at Harvard School of Psychology and Adjunct Professor of Neurology at Boston University Hospital) holds that mankind as a whole exhibits at least seven different types of intelligence, with all of us developing strength in one or more of these intelligences. They are:

- Verbal/linguistic intelligence is skill with written and spoken language, ranging from entertaining through to communicating ideas, solving crossword puzzles to writing books or poetry.
- Mathematical/logical intelligence implies logical or scientific thinking and step-by-step methodical exploration of patterns or sequences. Accountants, engineers and scientists could be expected to have this bent.
- Spatial intelligence is the ability to form three-dimensional mental models and manipulate them in one's mind. A navigator or an architect could be expected to have this in abundance.
- Musical intelligence was probably best exemplified by Beethoven who wrote some of his best work when stone deaf. His originality was no doubt partly due to the fact that while he couldn't hear his own music he couldn't hear or be influenced by anyone else's either.
- Bodily/kinaesthetic intelligence is exhibited by those who use their bodies, or parts of them, in work or play. People such as dancers, athletes and even surgeons and potters are adept at using their motor skills and hand/eye co-ordination.

Another two intelligences revolve around knowing yourself and knowing others. They are:

- Interpersonal intelligence, sensitivity to the moods and feelings of others; a politician or a priest could be expected to have this intelligence.
- Intrapersonal intelligence is the ability to know oneself correlatively and use the knowledge to live effectively and meaningfully.

To these we would add:
- Visual intelligence, which is shown by artists and designers, those who see the world in terms of shapes, colours and images.
- Naturist intelligence is the ability shown by those who have an instinct for the subtleties of their environment, who can recognise and utilise their skills in a natural environment. They can recognise species of plants and animals and instinctively feel comfortable in the great outdoors.

So where does all this lead? Gardner says, '… the purpose of school should be to develop intelligences and to help people reach vocational and avocational goals that are appropriate to their particular spectrum of intelligences. People who are helped to do so, I believe, feel more engaged and competent, and therefore more inclined to serve society in a constructive way.'

Similarly we believe we should all have access to the tools in business and in our private lives to better understand how our minds work and feel able to make our own contributions in 'brainstorming' or the development of ideas. Regardless of what our IQ is, we shouldn't feel intimidated around 'clever' people. Our intelligence type is more important for its ability to allow us to view the world differently.

The curse of 'confirmation bias'

While it's true that creative people are intelligent, it's not necessarily true that intelligent people are creative. The problem this creates manifests itself when organisations, commercial or social, attract and retain only like-minded, albeit bright, people. A kind of group-think ensues, what psychologists call 'confirmation bias'. If you live and work among the same people with similar opinions to your own, asking the same people the same questions will tend to get you the same answers. Only if organisations are refreshed and renewed with varied inputs will they be able to adapt and survive.

Unfortunately, in our current business climate, we seem to have adopted a short-term accounting bias: focussing on quarterly or annual financial targets, rather than innovative, long-term strategic solutions. Good ideas often have a life cycle or gestation period well outside traditional accounting parameters.

If you don't agree with this ask why the tops of many of the tallest buildings in our cities glow with the neon signs of banks, accounting firms and financial institutions — those who record and hoard, rather than those who make and do. Fifty or so years ago the biggest buildings were likely to be those of manufacturing companies, 100 years before that the tallest buildings were churches. This is an indication of what we honour and value in our society.

It's a 'sensible' world

It seems after the stock market crash in 1987, many imaginative entrepreneurs and business 'builders' were replaced by 'sensible' people, more cautious 'cost-cutters' whose focus was on trimming company costs. They were often uncomfortable dealing with innovation or 'intuitive' people and subjective 'stuff' that couldn't be measured. Similarly, ideas people became impatient with the 'sensibles' for stifling creativity.

Interestingly, the world seems to be run by 'sensible' people. Recent research in the United States indicates two-thirds of business graduates are 'sensible' types and the majority of all undergraduates are 'sensing' students (72 percent of over 16,000 freshmen at three state universities). Although the same survey reported that over 80 percent of national merit scholarship finalists, more than 90 percent of Rhodes Scholars and the majority of university faculties are intuitive.

So you can see we live in a world dominated by sensible people — there wouldn't be roads, bridges, buildings, cars, aeroplanes, hospitals and electricity grids without them. You certainly want your average airline pilot to be a 'sensible', otherwise he might decide to loop the loop just for the hell of it while you're enjoying your in-flight coffee. On the other hand, there would be little new in the way of discovery, adventure, philosophical insights, books, movies or music without 'intuitives'.

After a decade or so of downsizing, cost-cutting and focus on 'core' strategies in business we are at an economic crossroads. We have now become suspicious of clever accounting techniques following Enron, the dot.com boom and bust, and paper companies that relied on constant expansion or fanciful markets to build wealth. We need to be innovative to succeed.

Allowing dreamers to dream requires an enormous leap of faith on the part of those who run businesses. It can be a hit-and-miss affair. Non-intuitive people think that intuitive types who produce ideas are prone to goofing off, given half a chance. They don't understand how to work with them. Consequently, there is little reverence for ideas and ideas people — and formal corporate structures find people with green hair who don't keep normal hours to be a complete anathema.

For mutual respect to develop, symbiosis of 'intuitives' and 'sensibles' needs to be brought into the spotlight so that our interdependence can be recognised and the benefits of collaboration established.

There are a number of ways in which this co-operative relationship can be fostered, but an understanding of the respective strengths and weaknesses of various personality types is central to its acceptance.

'Know thyself'

Personality typing is a useful tool and learning to apply the theories of typology can be a fascinating and rewarding experience, but only if it is used as a development technique, not as a method for putting people into pigeon holes or excusing stereotypical behaviour.

Rather than pursuing the route of teaching everyone to be 'creative', we feel it is more appropriate to teach people to recognise what stitch they actually form in the rich tapestry of creativity. Are they weft or weave?

By understanding ourselves we can acknowledge whether we are writer or reader, innovator or implementer. There is no right or wrong place to be; we are what we are.

This book is our small contribution to an innovative climate that will nurture new ideas, to help people take advantage of their latent skills at home or at work, to produce business-building ideas that will be both meaningful and profitable and to generally have fun.

Dip in and dream on!

How to use this book

Problems cannot be solved by thinking within the framework in which the problems were created.

ALBERT EINSTEIN

This book is intended for the relief of writer's block and blank sheet syndrome: the awful scourge of not knowing where to start.

The truth is, when it comes to creativity and problem-solving, you can start anywhere. For example, this book is to be dipped into at any page, not read from cover to cover. If you are stuck for an idea and need to kickstart your creativity for whatever reason — from preparing next year's sales plan to finding a theme for the local school fair — open it at random and see if one of the 80 or so different 'thought starters' can trigger a brainwave. If your mind is still blank, keep flipping the pages until you find a catalyst.

If you feel some of the items are contradictory and only subtly different from others, you will be right. A paradox of problem-solving is exploration of opposites (see Do the opposite — flip, reverse, rotate, page 85). One may need to turn a problem completely on its head or alternatively twist it only slightly to see its other facets before a solution will reveal itself. There are no hard-and-fast rules — it all depends. A mark of intuitive creative people is their ability to be comfortable with paradox and ambiguity.

Leaving the beaten path opens up more possibilities. The game of rugby was invented when a boy picked up the ball and ran with it during a soccer game. Don't always assume a rote answer is correct. One and one does equal two in a mathematical sense, but two ones together is also eleven, if we forget our preconceived notions of arithmetic.

Go off the rails

*I don't give a damn for any man
who can spell a word only one way.*

MARK TWAIN

The need to find one 'right' answer is a bad habit. Finding that answer often stops us searching for other solutions.

Asking for several possible answers, rather than just one solution, unblocks people's minds. Ideas can then flow, bounce and build off one another.

Maybe we can blame our schooling for teaching us to want one correct answer to our questions. But most problems aren't like factual questions. They are unclear, complex and there is often more than one right way to solve them. Contrary to multiple-choice questions, the first answer that pops into our heads is not likely to be the best one. This is because our minds call up familiar, unoriginal examples faster than less typical ones.

Nemesis always follows hubris. The moment we get complacent and think we have produced an unbeatable product or attained an unassailable position is the moment we should sense danger. Life itself is a work in progress and improvements can always be made.

Improve

If there is a way to do it better ... find it.

THOMAS EDISON

The best ways to do things have been found. Right? Wrong. The best new products and services still don't exist.

Nothing can ever be seen as finished or complete. There is no final solution. Even if something works in today's rapidly changing world it probably won't be long before it's obsolete. We need to temper our discovery of a great idea with an understanding that it is a great idea today, but may not be tomorrow.

How often do we try to improve something that is already working well? When an idea is a success and we are happy with the results, we are less likely to check out other solutions to see if we could do better. Good ideas can be the enemy of better ones because we stop looking for alternatives. The idea gets a 'don't challenge' stamp on it from our thinking. The result is we are often left with yesterday's decisions long past their 'use-by' dates. This 'don't challenge' territory is fertile ground for finding new ideas because fewer people will be looking there.

We need to look further even when we have found a great idea. Looking for alternatives needs to be something we do as good practice even when we are satisfied with what we have. Be vigilant and ask: 'Why is it done this way and how can it be improved?' For example, make the issue, problem or idea more appealing, trendier, smarter, more sleek, cheaper, more efficient, feel better, sound better, taste better, smell better, smaller or more compact.

The wheel was invented after early man realised it was easier to roll a heavy object on a log than to drag it across the ground. A slice of log attached to an axle was found to be less cumbersome than a log, then followed the spoked wheel, the spoked wheel with a metal rim, the wheel with a solid rubber tyre and finally the pneumatic tyre. What's next? Is it a frictionless wheel? What about no wheel at all? Some modern trains work on magnetic repulsion, effectively floating with no ground contact at all.

Adapt and modify

Adaptability is not imitation. It means power of resistance and assimilation.

MAHATMA GANDHI

The reasonable man adapts himself to the world; the unreasonable one persists in trying to adapt the world to himself. Therefore all progress depends on the unreasonable man.

GEORGE BERNARD SHAW IN 'MAN AND SUPERMAN'

When did they modify the potato chip to make the French fry? How long did it take to put screw tops on beer bottles? These questions make you wonder how many great ideas are just sitting out there waiting to be found.

The ability to adapt and modify ideas will be the difference between a business's success and failure in the future. Remember, most ideas build from others. It is totally legitimate to adapt and modify. Fashion does this. What was once seen as an original and innovative solution in one area can be adapted, modified and applied to your problem or idea to solve or improve it.

Instead of starting from scratch, look for solutions that are already around and think how you can adapt them to your current problem. Ask: 'What could be adjusted, adapted or modified to fit?' For example, concrete is made stronger by putting steel rods inside it. Glass is tinted and toughened to be shatterproof depending on where it is going to be put.

Poetry is a great source of analogies. If you want to find inspiration or a source for a romantic allusion you need look no further than Shakespeare's sonnets. For example, 'Shall I compare thee to a summer's day ...' On the other hand, it's unlikely you'll find such inspiration in an automotive service manual.

Make analogies

All perception of truth is the detection of an analogy.

HENRY DAVID THOREAU

Life ... is like a grapefruit. It's orange and squishy, and has a few pips in it, and some folks have half a one for breakfast.

DOUGLAS ADAMS

Analogies link old knowledge to new. They help make the strange familiar by finding similarities in what seems to be dissimilar.

Watson and Crick were greatly helped in their discovery of the structure of DNA by seeing it as a spiral staircase. Today, a zip analogy helps schoolkids understand the basics of genetic biology.

Anything can become an analogy. For example: What greases the wheels towards your happiness? If creativity were a machine what would jam it?

How is ...

communication like radio waves?
the mind like a TV set?
cricket like life?
perception like the view from a window?
consciousness like the territory of the world?
fashion like architecture?
damage to the body like destruction of a landscape?
a negative person like the grit in your fingernails?

English road repairer Percy Shaw was out driving late one night in 1934. When he saw the reflection of a cat's eyes he thought of an idea that would revolutionise night-driving. Initially his suggestion to put reflective studs on the roads did not appeal to the powers that be. But during Second World War blackouts, car headlights had to be masked, making it difficult for drivers to see the road. Shaw's cat's eyes were introduced. Visible at ground level they didn't cast any light upwards, so they couldn't be seen by an enemy aircraft. This simple device is now used all over the world.

Rummage nature

We do not know one-thousandth of one percent of what nature has revealed to us.

ALBERT EINSTEIN

Nature is a catalyst for invention. After all, if the principle has worked and survived in nature for thousands of years why shouldn't it work for us? Looking at nature allows us to see how other life forms have solved problems and sometimes do things better than we do. In fact, there is a whole field of science, called bionics, specifically set up to borrow from nature.

- Plant seeds have taught us about aerodynamics and Velcro.
- Insect anatomy has helped us design robots, machines and diggers.
- The mechanics of the human eye inspired automatic focussing cameras.
- Natural camouflage in the animal kingdom has become a model for army uniforms.
- Radar came from studying the uses of reflected sound waves in bats.
- By studying dolphins, naval architects have been helped to understand the movement of ships' hulls through water.
- House paints have been designed to change colour between night and day to reflect or absorb heat based on the chameleon.
- Observing the sticking power of tree frogs due to their complex hexagonal patterned toe pads helped engineers improve the design of road-holding tyres in wet weather.
- Ball-and-socket joints on animals helped provide a model for machinery.
- Seeing dewdrops on leaves inspired the magnifying glass.
- The strength of bamboo inspired hollow steel cylinders.
- Nature's filters teach us about clarifying water, sewage and artificial kidneys.

You never know who you are talking to. Many good ideas have been inspired by chance encounters. It is said physician Edward Jenner got the idea of vaccinating against the scourge of smallpox from a milkmaid who told him that milkmaids who caught cowpox never get smallpox. In 1796, in an experiment which would never be sanctioned today, Jenner rubbed cowpox scabs into small incisions made in the arm of an eight-year-old boy. The boy was later exposed to smallpox and didn't become infected. Thus vaccination was born and through this method smallpox was eventually eradicated. So talk to different people, listen to taxi drivers — you never know what pearl you may pick up.

Know hearts and minds

To sway an audience, you must watch them as you speak.

C. KENT WRIGHT

The initial 'Star Wars' movie script was rejected 12 times by different studios. Many great ideas have been dumped as a result of decision-makers misunderstanding the hearts and minds of the audience.

Those who have no empathy with the audience tend to focus more on surface details, like nice materials, pictures and words. We need to imagine ourselves as the person who will eventually use our ideas. Single out your target and ignore everyone else.

Stay close to who it is that you want to accept your ideas. Get on buses. Sit in pubs. Talk to taxi drivers. To have great ideas we need to understand human psychology. Your idea could solve a universal human problem or conversely make people feel patronised, frustrated and misunderstood. Learn from people's preferences and cater to them. Understand what people want.

People want to ...

save time, money and energy;
have comfort, health, popularity, praise, fun and possessions;
be seen as smart, unique, important, attractive, in fashion and in the know;
feel competent, in control, clean, desirable and happy;
avoid effort, boredom, pain, discomfort, trouble, being excluded, loss, guilt, blame, danger, worry, confusion, incompetence and criticism.

It's a common trick of authors and advertising copywriters to picture a real person, often someone of their acquaintance, then write as if they are talking personally to that individual rather than an amorphous audience of 18-35-year-old females in a mid socio-economic group. It's like the difference between speaking in public and having a private conversation.

Picture the person

I bid him look into the lives of men as though into a mirror, and from others to take an example for himself.

TERENCE (ROMAN PLAYWRIGHT, C. 190 BC–158 BC)

Faceless statistics are worse than limiting; they are destructive when it comes to generating ideas.

Problems are much easier to understand if we have a specific example to focus on. Develop a mental picture of a person, rather than a number. What about that guy next to you on the bus?

For example, instead of starting a magazine for restless, bored males, aged 18 to 35, on an average income of X amount, concentrate on one bloke called Trev who's at the train station, buying a hot dog and thinking about quitting his job.

Interestingly, once we have met someone we often find it hard to recall what they look like. What we do remember is whether or not we like them and the feelings we get from being with them.

Accepted rules of art required artists to paint realistically and in perspective. The invention of photography made the 'recording' function of painting redundant. Photographs could record people and scenes far more accurately than a person could, no matter how skilled they were. Some painters then took art in new directions; they started to interpret impressions rather than record objects and a host of 'Modern Art' movements were born. Just because you can't always see both eyes, doesn't mean they aren't there.

Break rules and push boundaries

The golden rule is that there are no golden rules.

GEORGE BERNARD SHAW

Are your ideas innovative? More great ideas come from breaking rules and stretching boundaries than following them. Rules and boundaries provide something to push against — a springboard to leap from. Historically, Cézanne and Monet broke the rule of art and pushed a major boundary when they challenged the idea that painters had to represent reality as accurately as possible. Impressionism was born. Cubism, Surrealism and Dadaism soon followed. Artists kept on pushing boundaries, art became more abstract. In 1961, Matisse's 'Le Bateau' (The Boat) hung upside-down for two months in the Museum of Modern Art, New York — none of the 116,000 visitors had noticed.

We follow rules every day and give them little thought: be honest, pay your bills, don't use that word. While rules start for a reason, they often outlive their use-by date and continue because we don't challenge them. Rules can make us lazy. They also create sterile environments. The result: we limit our creativity. We need to challenge the rules created in our minds. Start by asking why. Why can't we use rude words? Why aren't power sockets at hip height? Why are there no windows inside houses?

Experts can be criticised for putting boundaries around subjects where none may exist: 'That won't work', 'Don't ask him', 'Fruit doesn't go with meat sauce', 'That colour wouldn't go', 'He won't read that'. Be wary of the pitfalls of an 'expert's' mindset.

Creativity can be enriched by collaboration. While some prefer to create in private, in truth there is 'no new thing under the sun' and testing your ideas on others can save pitfalls and strengthen concepts.

Bounce off others

The realisation that there are other points of view is the beginning of wisdom.

CHARLES CAMPBELL

People who aren't involved with the problem can provide new angles and fresh perspectives. Others can be rich sources of facts, opinions and information to spark off. By simply asking for someone else's perspective we can dig our thinking out of a rut, inspire and speed up our ideas.

Explain the difficulty. By explaining our perplexity to a good listener we can develop a better picture of what we are trying to solve, and aspects we may have missed or not considered can be pointed out.

Comedy writers often work in groups and advertising creative people usually work in teams of two: one writing the words and another conceiving the visual context to create a whole idea, its look and its sound.

Thomas Edison knew what he was talking about when he taught us that 'genius is 1 percent inspiration and 99 percent perspiration'. It is reported that he experimented with 1800 different prototypes before he came up with a successful electric light. But, in his determination, he didn't consider that he'd had a lot of failures — he just knew 1800 ways NOT to make a light bulb.

Fly in the face of failure

Adversity has the effect of eliciting talents which in prosperous circumstances would have lain dormant.

HORACE (65 BC–8 BC)

All great ideas require experimentation involving failure and error. We are all bound to fail sometimes. But each failure tells us something we did not know before until, finally, we know enough to succeed.

When we fail we draw on past experience. We try old ideas, and search familiar places where we have found successful ideas and solutions before. It is only when we have exhausted these options, however, that we really get our creative juices going.

For example, imagine you have locked your keys in the car. First you might try the door, then get frustrated. What you do next depends on your previous learning history. What has worked for you in the past? Maybe you search your pockets for a spare key, phone home, ring the breakdown service or try another key.

Still locked out of the car? You begin to think of options you may never have considered before: smash the side window, tell others in the parking lot and try their keys, or forget the car and walk home.

Allowing yourself to fail in a controlled, non-threatening, non-critical way, can generate fresh new ideas. One way to guarantee failure in a controlled way is to frame your problem as unsolvable: get your pet on TV news tonight, make a three-course meal for the price of a bus fare or build Noah's Ark.

The famous line attributed to Julius Caesar, 'Veni, vedi, vici', has been repeated so often it has indeed become a cliché. But imagine if you can twist it to have almost the opposite meaning. For example, 'I came, I saw, I concurred.' Take well-known clichés and turn them on their heads to derive new meanings.

Call on cliché

Let's have some new clichés.

SAMUEL GOLDWYN

A cliché is an over-used idea. So often people stop looking at clichés to find a solution. But hang on, isn't a place where others don't look a treasure trove for ideas?

Clichés by definition have the added benefit of being easily recognised. You can play on this and exploit the familiarity of a cliché in an unexpected way.

What clichés do you associate with the problem? How could you play on an old cliché to create a novel or original angle?

Yogi Berra, baseball star of the 1940s and 50s, gave the world some memorable aphorisms through distorted clichés: 'It ain't over till it's over', 'When you come to a fork in the road, take it' and 'It's déjà vu all over again'.

You can also find out the origin of clichés to give new inspiration or insight. For example, American poker players of the nineteenth century would pass a piece of buckshot from player to player to signify whose responsibility it was to deal, hence the term 'the buck stops here'. There was a tradition in USA slavery states in which slaves or free descendants would walk in a procession in pairs around a cake at a social gathering or party, the most graceful pair being awarded the cake as a prize. This gave us 'takes the cake' and 'a piece of cake'.

Queen Victoria gave her name to an era now synonymous with prim and prudish behaviour, an age of inflexible, stiff-upper-lip attitudes. How many other people or places are strongly identified with an era, a movement, or a style?

Pay homage

In the future everyone will be famous for 15 minutes.

ANDY WARHOL

People and images can become so well known that they can almost become sacred symbols of a style or era.

Make a home visit to some tired old icons. If managed well they can make a comeback just like disco and John Travolta. Icons have the advantage of being easily recognised. It's what you do with them that counts.

We can learn a lot about people, what's popular and successful by studying icons. What is it that makes some people or symbols attain icon status?

Napoleonic, Californian, Byzantine, Machiavellian are all eponymous adjectives evocative of an attitude, derived from the behaviour typical of those people or places.

Colours are great descriptors of moods. Is there a better way of expressing your intention than by using the vivid imagery inherent in colour? Will colour alone carry your idea?

Play with the palette

Marge, I can't wear a pink shirt to work. Everybody wears white shirts. I'm not popular enough to be different.

HOMER SIMPSON

Colour taps into core emotions. Whether we like something or not can depend on its colour. Many people, however, ignore or underestimate the power of colour perceptually, cross-culturally and emotionally. In fact, the only time most of us worry about colour is when selecting clothing or painting the living room. But colour can help us in far more fundamental ways than that.

Playing with hue and getting the tones right can be vital to any idea's development and success. What if all trees were red and fruit and flowers were green? Swapping, mixing and manipulating the colour of objects is an excellent creative technique. Some designers claim that colour plays a greater role than form. It can feed the other senses and create emotion, noise, rhythm and flavour. Some colours and colour relationships can be eye irritants, cause headaches, and wreak havoc with human vision. Other colours and colour combinations can soothe, calm, energise, heat and cool and generally make us feel better.

Our language is coloured with colour metaphors — blue moons, grey areas, silver linings, whitewash. People are coloured (rednecks, yellow-bellied, blue-blooded), situations are coloured (in the red or in the pink), our skills are coloured (green thumb), our emotions are coloured (green with envy, feeling blue), and even our behaviour can be coloured (golden handshakes, painting the town red).

What colour is your problem? What if it was a different colour? Darker, lighter, more pale, blond, metallic, frosted or fluoro?

> WHOA BIG FELLA! I THINK WE'VE COME TOO FAR!

New horizons and new experiences await the explorer. Since Marco Polo brought back silk from the Orient, many new developments have occurred after travellers have returned from foreign lands. The humble potato, so closely identified with Ireland, actually came back from South America with the conquistadors in the 16th century. Horace Greeley's dictum in the 1840s — 'Don't lounge in the cities ... Go west, before you are fitted for no life but that of the factory' — is still valid.

Go west

The vividness of strange places is one of the aphrodisiacs of writing.

JOHN LE CARRÉ

Many chance events, unanticipated connections and serendipitous discoveries have occurred while inventors, entrepreneurs, architects and designers were travelling. History is full of examples of famous people who have been stimulated by the mere switching of surroundings.

New places break our routine, jolt our awareness, excite our curiosity and refresh our creative spirit. If stuck for ideas, take a trip overseas or to a magazine shop or a friend's house. Maybe go on a half-day trip where you can browse around somewhere new.

Get lost in familiar places. Become a stranger in your own surroundings — you know how vividly you see a new town or a strange country when you first enter it. Ask what's going on. What sounds are you hearing, what smells do you pick up? Speculate about others around you. Where are they going? Notice the architecture, food and culture. Some places elicit strong feelings because of the momentous events that have occurred there.

Travel helps convert the usual to the unusual. We notice things we otherwise ignore. New environments have unfamiliar colours, textures, tastes and smells. Everyday objects such as signs, shops, money and phone booths stand out and appear fresh.

Merely deciding to travel is not enough. You need to actively participate. Let your interests drive you to unusual places, exhibitions, movies or strange parts of town.

As the words of the old song say, 'The thigh bone's connected to the knee bone, the knee bone's connected to the leg bone ...' — everything's connected to everything else. People and planets live and die and their atoms are merely reconstituted in different molecular combinations. Astronomer Carl Sagan once said, 'In order to make an apple pie from scratch, you must first create the universe.'

Make connections

To develop a complete mind: study the science of art; study the art of science. Learn how to see. Realise that everything connects to everything else.

LEONARDO DA VINCI

Iron is present in stars, the soil, the food we eat and also in our blood. One of the paths to creativity is understanding that everything is related. Nothing really stands completely apart. Making connections opens our minds to new ideas as our imagination leaps to fill the gaps. We need to constantly remind ourselves to look at how things are related because our minds naturally tend to see how things differ.

Forcing relationships between things is a commonly recommended creativity technique. This involves blindly and randomly opening a book, magazine, thesaurus or dictionary and asking how your problem is like something you randomly pick, like a fridge, phone or car.

In reality, however, people tend to pick what they wish to connect their issue or problem with. Self-selecting the themes or objects you'd like to connect your problem to can be less shallow and more intrinsically motivating. For example, if you had a phrase, postcard or a theory you liked you could spend time imagining how it could be connected to your problem.

How would a boxing match be fought if the boxers came out smiling instead of swinging? The juxtaposition of elements we don't normally associate can create unexpected surprise.

Contrast

Somebody who thinks logically is a nice contrast to the real world.
ANONYMOUS

Juxtaposition and contrast can be used to expand our thinking by revealing unexpected similarities or major differences.

Compare: How is the problem like X?
Contrast: Why is it not?

There are many things we can contrast:
- People (Rich? Poor?)
- Ages (Young? Old?)
- Styles (Modern? Post-modern?)
- Problems (Passive? Aggressive?)
- Inventions (Practical? Impractical?)
- Sizes (Big? Small?)
- Colours (Blue? Green?)
- Shapes (Sharp? Blunt?)
- Places (Desert? Ocean?).

What would a world of no consequences be like? If we didn't save our money yet could still make a withdrawal from the bank, what would that do to economics? So many actions result in effects that are unintended. Try and think through the levels of consequences. Remember Murphy's Law. Anything that can go wrong will.

Consider consequences

There are in nature neither rewards nor punishments, there are consequences.

ROBERT INGERSOLL

Imagining all the possible outcomes of a problem can help us have ideas. For example, when smoking was banned inside restaurants one of the consequences was that people still wanted somewhere to go to smoke, so some smart person thought of cigar bars while others thought of how they could get more seats outside their restaurants. Many great ideas are missed because people neglect thinking about all the possible consequences of their decisions.

Consider the array of consequences surrounding a problem and allow them to shape your thinking. Imagine yourself at the end state and then work backwards. Play with some of the consequences. What would life be like without the service, problem or product? What would replace it? What if things didn't change? What if things got worse?

Idealise. Sometimes we all get so caught up in the problem that we forget about what we want as the ideal solution. Start by imagining the perfect solution, then make comparisons with what you have now. This helps us identify what gets in the way. It gives us a goal and something to aspire to. For example, what would be your ideal working environment? What would be the best, most perfect outcome? What would life be like if the issue was no longer a problem for anyone? How would life be different? How would you be able to tell things had changed around you? What gets in the way of getting there? If we promise something, can we deliver?

A notepad by the bed or a small dictaphone can be priceless for their ability to capture our thoughts as they occur. How many times have we woken at night and instructed ourselves to remember a thought so profound we 'know' it will still be there in the morning, only to find it has slipped into the mists of forgotten dreams?

Catch your thoughts

A man would do well to carry a pencil in his pocket and write down the thoughts of the moment. Those that come unsought are commonly the most valuable and should be secured, because they seldom return.

FRANCIS BACON

We can often recall the time and place we had an idea but not the idea itself.

How good is your memory? Most people only remember 50 percent of what they are told and that's only after the first hour. Memory for new material declines steadily after that. Many profitable ideas are lost because of the simple act of forgetting.

Ideas are unpredictable and can occur anywhere any time. In the middle of the night, on beaches, in planes, hotels and cafés, and sometimes at your desk. As a general rule, acknowledge that ideas are fragile and fleeting and need to be recorded in some way or else they may disappear forever.

When you have an idea, wherever you are, if it appeals to you, make a note of it. Jot it down, take a photo or write on your sleeve. You will be astounded weeks and even years later when you read over your notes at all the ideas you had that you've forgotten.

Writers, artists and designers often have ideas they have kept aside for years just waiting for an opportunity to be used.

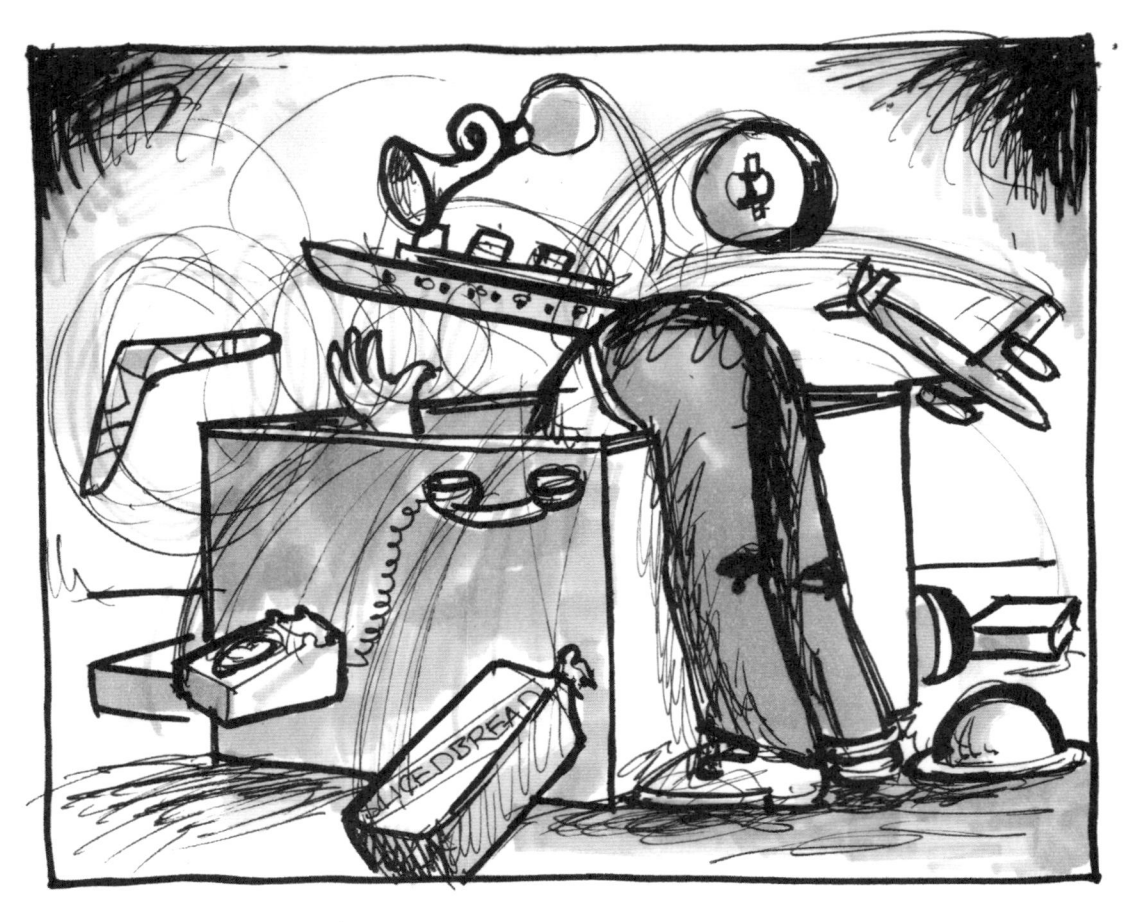

Creative people are not often the tidiest. Their attics and garages are likely to contain an eclectic cache of items, kept on the basis that they never know when that 'thing' might come in handy. The most fascinating workshops and sheds are those of tinkerers and inventors.

Start hoarding

To invent, you need a good imagination and a pile of junk.

THOMAS A. EDISON

Make a habit of noticing and even scrutinising ideas that others have used successfully. Read, remember, record and collect. Postcards, books, videos, souvenirs, cartoons, photos, jokes, quotes, trophies, cards, ornaments, observations and conversations can all fill your idea pool.

Become the world's biggest hoarder! If you like something, keep it. Trust what draws your attention. Don't worry about justifying your choices with logic. Creative people have drawers or walls filled with random objects that grabbed their attention, some they never use. Others find a use years later. Collected objects can trigger other idea techniques. For example, an object collected on holiday can encourage your mind to return to a faraway place, creating a new 'head space'. Trinkets you kept from school could trigger you to think like a kid. Old gifts might start you thinking about a friend and what they might have to say about your problem or issue.

Even if an item is never used, the mere act of pondering, handling and mentally chewing can work like good nutrients to nourish your mind.

> IT'S MY NEW FISH-HEAD, CABBAGE AND ICECREAM DISH....
>
> WHAT DO YOU CALL IT?
>
> AWFUL!

Sports teams win when new combinations of moves or players take the opposition by surprise. We relish the thrill of new combinations — if they're successful, of course.

Some of the best cuisine comes from new combinations of flavours or ingredients.

Combine

Snowflakes are one of nature's most fragile things, but just look what they can do when they stick together.

VISTA KELLY

Stars shine because two atoms of hydrogen combine to make helium. Similarly, our mind fires when facts meld to create unexpected insights. Many ideas are based on combining a number of elements into one idea. Often the combination of ideas can create something greater than the parts.

Great chefs know that by combining different flavours they can create new recipes. Engineers know about how certain metals when combined can be made stronger. Similarly, industrial designers know how synthetic fibers are made tougher by mixing ingredients. And more recently we have seen how cartoonists have found success by mixing ideas from martial arts, renaissance and Zen to create the successful 'Teenage Mutant Ninja Turtles'.

But it's not just products that are born out of combining elements. People problems can also be solved by merging ideas. For example, work is often made more enjoyable by combining it with elements of leisure such as bringing pets to work, using scooters to get around the office or wearing weekend clothes on week days. And often the only way to get competing groups of kids to co-operate is if they are united towards a single goal.

EINSTEIN'S DOODLE PAD

Putting random thoughts on paper in diagrammatic form can help solve many problems. Somehow, no matter how crudely, putting numbers, drawings or sketches on paper takes them out of the mental ether and makes them real. Doodling enables thoughts to be pushed and prodded into new sequences, shapes and forms.

Drawings, diagrams and doodles

Painting is just another way of keeping a diary.

PABLO PICASSO

It is not uncommon for people with a mental block to grab a pen and paper and instinctively start doodling or sketching. It is almost as if when stuck for ideas, we are programmed to try and use more visual images. In fact, being able to see your problem or issue both verbally and diagrammatically is thought to be a factor of genius. Edison, Einstein and da Vinci used diagrams. Darwin and Beethoven used sketchbooks. Words can become just secondary notes.

The mind reacts more creatively to pictures than words because drawing bypasses thought and language, opening up more avenues to our thinking. Verbalising can also disrupt our intuitive understanding and act like noise, blocking the more subtle and less clear insights from our unconscious.

Don't hesitate to get out a pen and paper and draw what you're thinking, even if it's arrows and stick figures. Could your problem be a model, diagram or three-dimensional figure?

> WE CAME FROM THE SAME SINGLE CELL ORGANISMS — BUT THEY MUTATED VERY BADLY.

All life began in the primordial ooze, but through a series of mutations different life forms took different evolutionary paths. Some adapted better than others. For instance, fish are better adapted to their environment than we are to ours — after all, they don't have to wear clothes or build houses. Look for the key characteristics of an object or an idea that makes it different from others, then focus or exaggerate that point to help define its uniqueness.

Distort and mutate

*Facts, or what a man believes to be facts, are always delightful ...
Get your facts first, and ... then you can distort 'em
as much as you please.*

MARK TWAIN

Distorted appearances shock and amuse us. Cartoonists play on distortion. For example, they give females more curves to make them look sexier. Animals get bigger heads to make them look cuter. Bad guys get bumpy noses to make them scarier.

So another way to see a problem in a different way is to distort, mutate, elongate, stretch, flatten, inflate, bend and twist it.

Mutations can produce beneficial results. This idea has parallels in nature with genetic mutations. While over 95 percent fail, we need to remember five percent succeed and are an improvement on what was around before — that is how evolutionary progress is said to occur.

> I THOUGHT I WAS MAKING PUMPKIN SOUP – BUT I MUST HAVE GOT THE FORMULA WRONG....

As the alchemists of old tried to synthesise gold by mixing up base metals, is there a new way to reassemble the component parts of your problem to find another solution?
Can it be broken down into bite-sized chunks and reassembled in other ways? Will it still do the same job?

Divvy up

The chemical analysis of a cup of soup should not be expected to taste like the soup.

ALBERT EINSTEIN

Subtle changes to the ingredients can create a brand new recipe. Break a subject into assets or features, then study the parts. Listing attributes can help if you need to find new ways to extend, modify or improve a product or service. This technique can be useful if you question each attribute's function and value. Ask what is the point and usefulness of the separate parts. Are they still necessary? Next, think in what ways each could be changed, adjusted, reassociated or improved.

For example, you are asked to design a new office building for yourself and your peers. Break up the components of the problem to consider aspects such as the theme, size, location, architecture, divisions, interiors, furniture, colours and fixtures. These sections can again be subdivided into a whole series of options; e.g. location may include a hill, the main road, outside the city, at the beach or on the top floor of a building.

"THE PRESENT LETTER IS A LONG ONE, SIMPLY BECAUSE I HAD NO LEISURE TO MAKE IT SHORTER."

It's easier to write a long report than a short one. Condensing an idea to its essential elements requires mental rigour and confidence. French philosopher and mathematician Blaise Pascal gave us an immortal line: 'The present letter is a long one simply because I had no leisure to make it shorter.'

Extract the essence

Anybody can have ideas — the difficulty is to express them without squandering a quire of paper on an idea that ought to be reduced to one glittering paragraph.

MARK TWAIN

To shift our thinking from preconceived barriers, we need to find the overall essence of the subject. If we were asked to design a new electric jug most of us would get stuck by focussing only on the jugs we've already seen. So instead ask: 'What is the essential purpose of the jug?' The answer: 'To boil water.' Now plastic and other non-jug-type factors can come into our thinking.

For example:
- The purpose of a glass is to hold liquid so we can drink it.
- The purpose of a chair is to support our bodies in an upright position.
- Photographs are about capturing time.
- Can-openers are for getting the contents out of a can.
- Telephones are a means of communication.
- Our homes are personalised shelters.
- Cars are about transport.

Make the problem, product or service one sentence, phrase, a headline, poster, a title, one key word, one symbol or one synonym. Concentrate on expressing what's vital. What differentiates it? What are the fundamental bare bones of the problem?

In subjective matters answers are seldom clear but, if we wait for certainty, chances of success can be lost. It always pays to ask the questions 'What is the worst thing that could happen? What is the very best thing?' It's surprising how often, by asking these questions, our reluctance to act is unblocked. What are the extremes? How good can it be? How bad?

Turn up the heat

The only way to discover the limits of the possible is to go beyond them into the impossible.
ARTHUR C. CLARKE, 'TECHNOLOGY AND THE FUTURE'

To be pleased with one's limits is a wretched state.
JOHANN WOLFGANG VON GOETHE

Some problem-solvers are like particle physicists. They think that to really get to grips with a problem it needs to be put under extreme pressure. Observing a problem or issue being pushed to its limits can open up new avenues as well as reveal limitations.

For example, let's look at the problem of staff retention. What if a couple of staff were leaving? What if everyone wanted to leave? Do these two extremes get you to look at the problem differently? Would you behave differently? Would different issues arise? Can your answers help with the original problem of trying to keep staff?

Extend the problem in each direction as far as you can. How far can you go and to what extreme? What if the problem was significantly worse than it is now?

Make it the highest, longest, toughest, fastest, biggest, slowest, worst, ugliest or least reliable. What if everyone had it? What if everyone did it? What would life be like if the problem grew to mammoth proportions? What if the whole organisation, country or the whole world wanted it?

Some people are kinaesthetic learners. They learn by manipulating objects and by physical experience. They'd rather visit a place than watch a documentary on Discovery channel; to them there's nothing like being there. You would have to wonder, if Archimedes wasn't a kinaesthetic learner, would he still have had his 'Eureka!' moment in discovering the principle of water displacement?

Experience

You will think me lamentably crude: my experience of life has been drawn from life itself.

MAX BEERBOHM, 'ZULEIKA DOBSON'

Dive in, saturate, immerse, touch, feel, eat, observe, surround, live, sit beside, experience and play with the problem.

Research shows first-hand experience with the problem or issue is better than our imagination alone for jolting creative ideas. Shift it around or lie under it. Whatever it is, try to encounter the problem or issue in original ways if you can — not just in the way everyone else has.

And if we have already spent time with the problem, service or product, maybe we need to think about how we can experience it in even more tangential ways. For example, eat the competition's lunch, look at another person's photos of the problem or read their notes.

'From out of the mouths of babes and fools ...' goes the old saying. The perennial question 'Why?' that young children ask is probably one of the most profound. It should be answered, if only to encourage the child's curiosity. It underscores Aristotle's view: 'All men by nature desire to know.' In any problem-solving group, if we all think the same some of us are unnecessary. Three-year-old Emma, a young girl of our acquaintance, asked her father, 'Daddy, do clouds have wheels?' When told 'No', she asked, 'How do they land?'

Dare to be naïve

Each thing we see hides something else we want to see.

RENÉ MAGRITTE

Experience may help solve a problem but the opposite is also true — there is a lot to be said for remaining ignorant. Being unaware of the barriers means the potential solution pool you swim in is less restricted.

The reason kids have such active imaginations is because they haven't experienced much. As adults we often think we 'know' so we stop imagining.

Naturally, those not directly involved in a problem don't feel swamped by it either. They have what's been called the 'outsider's advantage'. Einstein was a mathematician not a physicist, the Wright brothers were bike mechanics, Louis Pasteur was a medical doctor, the ballpoint pen was invented by a sculptor, Kodachrome film was developed by a musician and the Coca Cola logo was designed by an accountant.

If you remain content to look at what others have tried, their successes and failures, you may end up getting stuck where everyone else has got stuck. Sooner or later you're going to have to loose your moorings, say goodbye to everyone on the shore and sail the boat on your own.

Not knowing will make your thinking unjaded and fresh. There will always be plenty of 'experienced' people to tell you why your ideas won't work.

The invention of synthetic turf means sports can be played outdoors in all-weather conditions. And what do they say about plastic flowers? They are 'the gift that goes on giving'.

Falsify

Every man is a borrower and a mimic, life is theatrical and literature a quotation.

RALPH WALDO EMERSON, 'SOCIETY AND SOLITUDE'

Play with what's false and what's real. Good ideas are often the result of mimicking. This is not just limited to the realms of furniture and jewellery.

Falsifying things can save time and money. For example, shop owners can save themselves having to carry their goods in and out each day by painting pictures of their wares on the wall outside their shops. And false rocks and glass help prevent injuries in movies and TV shows.

Although most of us don't like plastic grass or stick-on brick tiles and still prefer our own teeth, people don't always want the real thing. Kids prefer toy cars and plastic baby dolls. Artificial plants mean office staff don't need to remember to do any watering.

We all have our dark side. Sometimes if we act out of character we can blame it on our alter ego. Knowing what makes our mischievous half appear and when allows us to avoid certain situations and help control our behaviour.

Blame it on Bob

Blame someone else and get on with your life.

ALAN WOODS

So it was Bob who made you eat all that chocolate, Sid who made you forget to put petrol in the car and Marge who made you spend all your savings?

Our problems can be solved much faster if we don't feel blamed. Externalising is a creative way to get us talking to each other more objectively.

For example, do you sleep too much? Take too many drugs? Drink till you're plastered? Overeat? Whatever you do, let's call your problem Bob. When did Bob introduce himself to you? What did he do to entice you into a relationship with him? When are your best times together? What upsets him and makes him jealous? When do you not get on so well? When are you able to be distant from him? What feeds Bob? What starves him? Has your relationship improved lately? Why? Or why not?

Bob tends to feed off things like bad feelings, insecurities and isolation. If everyone works together to fight Bob using support, non-blaming and finding more healthy alternatives to compete with him, he can often be made to fade away.

Father Christmas is an excellent positive external explanation of how we get presents. Parents can use this to their advantage to work with their children to bring out the best behaviour: 'If you tidy your room, Santa will be able to see how much you deserve that bicycle you want.'

One definition of creativity is 'making the familiar strange and the strange familiar'.

Pablo Picasso exemplified this when he took two very familiar objects — a bicycle seat and a set of handlebars — and by welding them together made 'Bull's Head', a famous piece now in a Barcelona museum. Picasso made us see two everyday objects in a totally different way.

Make the familiar strange

Familiarity reduces the greatness of things.

SENECA (4 BC–65 AD)

Challenging our view of what's familiar can stretch our imagination. Have you ever looked at something familiar for a long time and really studied it? Strange thoughts can come to mind. Try it. Think about this thing you take for granted. Consider what else it could mean.

When people and ideas become familiar we stop thinking about them. Familiarity can literally hide great ideas from us. Upsetting our thinking by seeing things as strange, odd or problematic, however, can spark our thoughts and reignite our minds. We need to sometimes see the usual as unusual.

> IS THAT THE ELECTRIC CO? NO DOUBT THIS IS MORE IMPORTANT TO ME THAN TO YOU — BUT I WANT IT FIXED — AND SOON!!

To get any problem solved, make sure that the person with most to gain or lose is in charge. Don't delegate to someone who doesn't really care — there is no incentive for them to succeed. People respond best to real and immediate needs; abstract, remote problems don't carry the same urgency. Necessity is the mother of invention.

Love it or shove it

A hunch is creativity trying to tell you something.

FRANK CAPRA

The best ideas are often brought to life by emotion. Our feelings drive our work. What inspires us leads us to have great ideas. If you are cynical your ideas will be restricted.

The image of the best ideas stemming from rational, objective problem-solvers is a myth. Emotionally involved thinkers are increasingly seen as the innovators of tomorrow.

Try to find something you like about the problem you are trying to solve. What fuels your motivation may not necessarily be related to the final outcome, but if you can't find a legitimate emotional reason why you want the problem solved, then maybe you are not the best person for the job.

Make a point of being alert to your feelings and hunches — don't discard them. Try the overnight test. Listen to the problem, sleep on it and the pieces that survive in the morning are probably what you have an emotional attachment to (see Sleep On It, page 187).

Dig deep to find something about the problem or product that is exciting or interesting, otherwise you'll risk being trite. Shallow conceptual gymnastics will result if you're not deeply committed to the problem or issue. To get in the mood read about or talk to those who are inspired by it.

The biggest breakthroughs are often made by people working outside the field in question. Einstein was a lowly patent clerk when he developed his theory of relativity, the electric chair was invented by a dentist and the electric fence was invented when a New Zealand farmer attached wires to his car battery to discourage a horse from rubbing against his shiny new car. Generalists can often see more sides to a problem than specialists.

Swap hats

Most advances in science come when a person for one reason or another is forced to change fields.

PETER BURDEN

Spotting a successful idea in one field and applying it to another often leads to groundbreaking results. So why don't people do it more often?

Every field has a focus and its own way of dealing with problems. Plumbers see pipes, electricians see wires, hairdressers see haircuts, and artists see angles, perspectives and colour.

Often we get too locked into a field or we just never get the opportunity to step into another area and see how our concepts and theories might be adapted and applied. For example, what is a river to a geologist may be veins to a surgeon, irrigation to a farmer, or a branching tree to a botanist. Heart surgeons swap bad pipes for better ones in the same body. How could you swap some people for others in your organisation?

Develop an eye for seeing solutions in one area and applying them to another. Put on someone else's hat. Pretend to be an accountant, anthropologist, architect, bricklayer, biologist, dancer, gardener, mechanic, manager, teacher, rubbish collector, soldier, dentist, geologist, parent, poet, politician, surgeon or alien. How would they solve the problem?

The marketing penny dropped at Stanley Tools when someone realised the average home handyman was less interested in the drill than the hole: 'At Stanley, we don't sell drills. We sell holes.'

'At last', says the consumer, 'someone understands my problem.' That's a company consumers can have a relationship with. Stanley has built a brand that people can trust and has broken the cycle of having to yell 'low price' louder than the competition.

Do the opposite — flip, reverse, rotate

Any intelligent fool can make things bigger, more complex and more violent. It takes a touch of genius — and a lot of courage — to move in the opposite direction.

E. F. SCHUMACHER

What are you thinking about? What if the opposite were true? Flip the problem, reverse it, turn it upside down, inside out, roll it backwards, approach it from behind, invert it, rotate it, look at the other side or go underneath it.

Reversing everyday assumptions can challenge our thinking and produce different trains of thought. For example: Eskimos use refrigerators to keep food from freezing.

Reversals allow you to look at conventional things in a new way. For example, do you have a problem, or does the problem have you? To discover how you might continue your company's success explore how you might stop it. To understand why some people have a problem look at those who don't. Or to find out how to sell more ask: 'How could we sell less?' Or look at politics — rather than trying to make the leader look good sometimes the strategy is to focus on making the other guys look bad.

Does the news help us understand what's going on in the world or could it be blocking our understanding? Similarly, when looking at what can be done to improve your creativity take a note of what kills it.

They say some people are born with a microscope and some with a telescope. Make sure your focal length is right when you are examining a problem. If it's all a blur you are probably too close. If you can't see the finer points you may be too far away. Are you seeing the wood or the trees?

Adjust the focus

You can't depend on your eyes when your imagination is out of focus.

MARK TWAIN

One way to jam your thinking is to fill it with everything at once. Experiment by focussing on one thing at a time. For example, notice all red things within your view. Notice people who leave and those who stay. Spot all the different types of fences people have as you drive by. Take a different focus by using selective perception.

Don't let the problem direct your focus because the solutions may lie elsewhere. For example, if you were considering a design for a better chair notice people who stand. You may get better ideas about what's comfortable from talking to them.

An example of needing to discover the correct focal length can be found with the novelty pictures composed of multi-coloured dots or tiny geometric shapes. These appear to be a kaleidoscopic blur at first but if you stare at them long enough, with eyes slightly out of focus, they reveal three-dimensional images of birds, dragons and other objects.

A few years ago in a port city on the south coast of England was an old pub called 'Dick Turpins' — proudly emblazoned on the window were signs advertising the establishment as a Pizzeria and Karaoke Bar.

Globalise

... centres of creativity tend to be at the intersections of different cultures, where beliefs, lifestyles and knowledge mingle and allow individuals to see new combinations of ideas with greater ease.

MIHALY CZIKSZENTMIHALYI, 'CREATIVITY FLOW AND THE PSYCHOLOGY OF DISCOVERY AND INVENTION'

It seems we now have four sizes: small, medium, large and global. Sharing global values is becoming a way of life. And globalising can change your perspective so that you can look at your problem in a new light.

What would happen if your problem occurred elsewhere? Could your solution fit in comfortably anywhere? Can your ideas move between countries with ease? Across religions, cultures and customs? What would a 13-year-old Chinese girl have to say? Or a New York taxi driver?

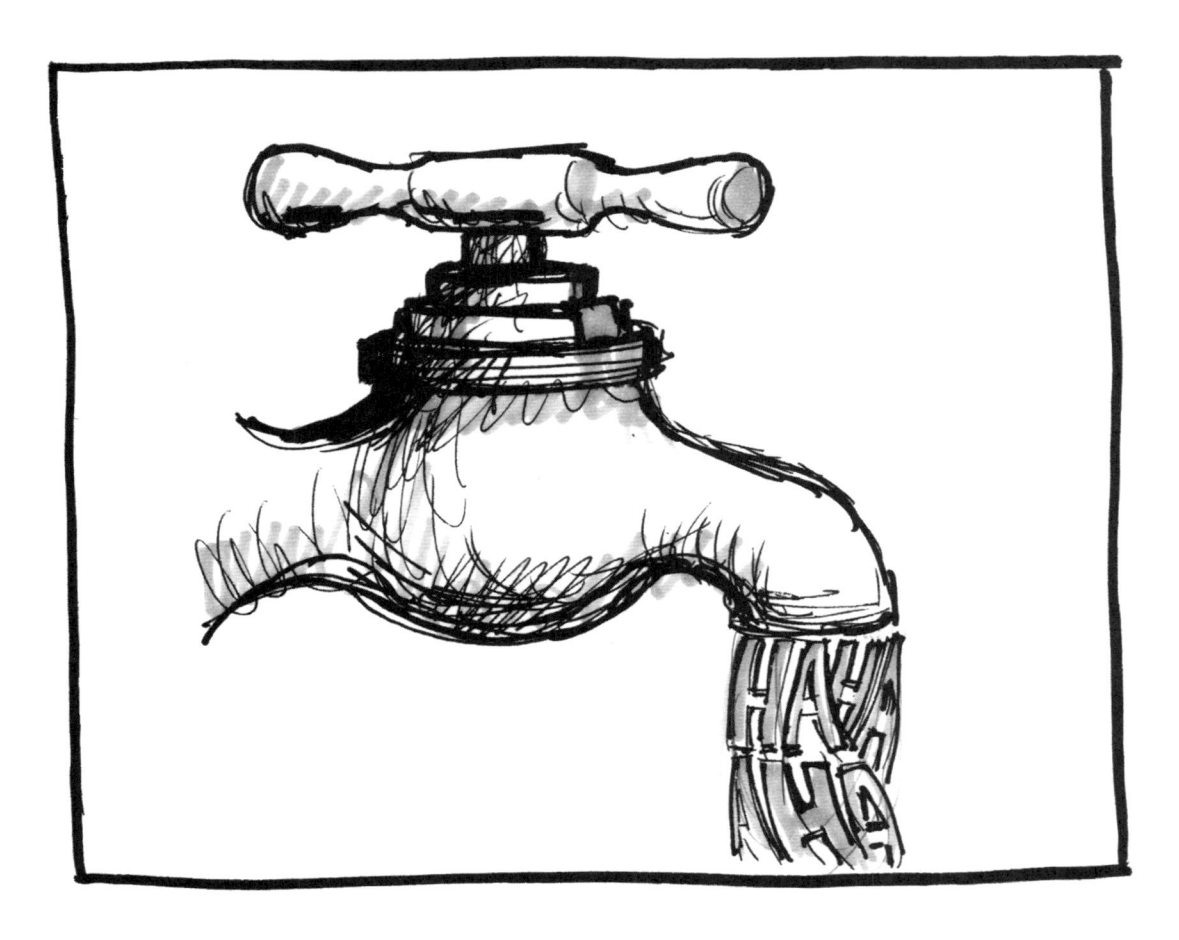

'Humour is a funny thing ...'
Anonymous

Tap humour

Imagination was given to man to compensate him for what he is not. A sense of humour was provided to console him for what he is.

HORACE WALPOLE

Having ideas is not a grim business. Great ideas can start from people joking around. What's funny about your problem or issue? Humour, wit and creativity are cousins. The structures that lead to wit can also lead to significant creative breakthroughs.

Humour surprises us by taking our thinking in a different direction from where it was going. It releases us from the brain's natural desire to find a pattern. It sets us off in one direction, gives us an expectation and then changes tack.

Humour can also be used as a barometer of our own attitudes, personalities and prejudices. It can be a short cut to what is profound and contain edited versions of great truths. Humour can lead us to a deeper level of understanding.

We are more likely to break boundaries when poking fun at a problem. It disarms feelings of self-consciousness. Humour also renews our energy, creates a playful state of mind and opens us up to see things we might otherwise ignore.

If our planet were to be invaded by aliens who could speak English, what would they call it? Earth may not be the most obvious name since it is nearly three-quarters covered in water and looks blue when seen from outer space. Ours is a living language; new words are entering our lexicon daily.

Swelligantify

If lawyers are disbarred and clergymen defrocked, doesn't it follow that electricians can be delighted, musicians denoted, cowboys deranged, tree surgeons debarked and dry-cleaners depressed?

INTERNET JOKE

Don't allow language to restrict what you wish to express. If you like, make up words and rename everyday things. Making up words is how language develops. Finding a new word can help us establish the essence of what we are trying to articulate. Rich Hall in his book *Sniglets* came up with many examples of made-up words:

Carperpetuation *(kar' pur pet u a shun), n.: The act, when vacuuming, of running over a string at least a dozen times, reaching over and picking it up, examining it, then putting it back down to give the vacuum one more chance.*

Snacktrek, *n.: The peculiar habit, when searching for a snack, of constantly returning to the refrigerator in hopes that something new will have materialised.*

Consider how appropriate existing names are or find out where names come from. The ceremony where they give out statuettes is called the Oscars because in 1931 Margaret Herrick spotted a copy of one and said: 'Why, he looks just like my Uncle Oscar.'

New words are being created all the time — Bazillion, relaxification, giganimous and swelligant are words we understand but can't find in any dictionary. One trick to find new names is to select from a completely different industry or category. This is how sports jargon and military language make it into the everyday world. For example, 'on the back foot', 'on a sticky wicket', 'knock-out', 'pull the punches', or 'par for the course'. Don't just leave it to academics to find new labels.

'One man's meat is another man's poison' is an oft-repeated saying. If there is something about your life or job that irks you, turn it to advantage by looking at it in a different way. If you are tired of attending endless, non-productive meetings, make a game of it.

Invent from irritation

We are continually faced with a series of great opportunities brilliantly disguised as insoluble problems.

JOHN W. GARDNER

People's irritations are an excellent source of ideas. Many everyday hassles are, however, so common that we no longer notice them, like getting out of bed to turn the lights off, waiting for paint to dry, remembering to return a video and putting the rubbish out on the right day. Inventions come from people recognising and understanding a need they or others have had.

Consider the people who invented bum bags for cyclists. They realised that everyone without pockets had a similar problem with what to do with little things like loose change. There was suddenly so much demand for these the world could not meet the supply.

What are some common irritations people have?

- Getting stuck in traffic
- Not being able to afford a holiday
- Loneliness
- Nagging relatives
- Second-hand cigarette smoke
- Kids addicted to the Internet
- Boring meetings
- Too much to read
- Telemarketers
- Nasty neighbours

Consider how life could be made easier and simpler. What do people need? What do people complain about?

Play it by ear, student bodies, spin doctors, right as rain, or getting taken to the cleaners. What would happen if these phrases were taken literally?

Go literal

If you get married holding an antenna in your hand is the reception any better?

EUGENE RUANE

A common ideas technique used in advertising, charades and comedy is to take things literally. Our language can play many tricks on us. A key element of humour can be found in the literal interpretation of phrases or commands. And as you will find in many of the triggers to creativity in this book the element of surprise inherent in humour can set our minds off on lots of new paths. If we laugh as we work the joy of discovery is heightened and enhanced. We become engrossed in the task, finding more and more possibilities because it's so enjoyable.

If you tell someone to 'take a hike' do you expect them to head for the hills or just discreetly remove themselves from your sight? How worried would you be if they took you literally? It makes you realise how often we use metaphor and hyperbole in everyday speech without meaning to be taken at face value.

If you want to know what colours will work together, go to nature not a paint colour chart. Watch a sunset. If the colours of approaching dusk work in the sky, chances are they'll work in your colour scheme. Industrial artefacts can often be turned to domestic use. A stainless-steel sieve could be turned into a lampshade. Maybe a jeweller can craft a piece in the form of a tropical fish.

Look in the 'wrong' place

I may not have gone where I intended to go, but I think I have ended up where I intended to be.

DOUGLAS ADAMS

Our minds tend to get stuck in certain places. We start to accept familiar and adequate solutions when we could discover much better ones if we searched wider afield and persevered.

For example:
- Read 'National Geographic' to find ideas for fabric designs.
- Read old science fiction books for invention ideas.
- Go to the beach to get ideas for jewellery.
- Look at outdoor furniture for indoors.
- Get colours for paint from tropical birds and fish.

Dimitri Mendeleev developed the periodic table of elements by playing around with a pack of cards; Columbus 'discovered' the Americas while searching for India; there is an interior design trend for using industrial items in domestic situations. Think about where you wouldn't expect to find an answer, but possibly could.

In your mind's eye what do you see your problem morphing into? When creative people are asked whether, if stuck between a rock and a hard place, they'd rather be closer to the rock or the hard place, they tend to pick the hard place because in their minds it can morph into something safe, such as an oil-drilling platform with a rescue helicopter. In the well-known 1970s TV programme 'The Rise and Fall of Reginald Perrin', Reggie's mother-in-law was morphed into a mud-caked hippo.

Metamorph

Doctor David Banner, physician, scientist, was searching for a way to tap into the hidden strengths that all humans have. Then an accidental overdose of gamma radiation alters his body chemistry. And now, when David Banner grows angry or outraged, a startling metamorphosis occurs ...

OPENING VOICEOVER FOR 'INCREDIBLE HULK' TV SERIES

'Animorphs' is a TV series about kids who can 'morph' into any animal they like. Graphic technology has made this show possible. Can you morph your problem into something else? Recent movies such as 'Men In Black' and 'Matrix' have elevated morphing to an art form. There are computer programmes available that allow photographs to be morphed, so that you can see a face ageing before your eyes or see one face changing into another by the gradual distorting of features. In nature, morphing can be witnessed as a chrysalis turns into a beautiful butterfly.

The idea behind a metamorphosis is that it needs to look 50 percent like the previous frame and 50 percent like the next frame. How can the perfect stages of a metamorphosis help you with your problem? If it involves change how could it be seamless? Can your problem be broken down into a series of smooth stages? Sales people break down the introduction of a new product into a series of stages to help build tension and suspense. How many frames or stages would it require to morph your problem into something else?

When fishing off the rocks a well-known fishing guide always recommended, 'Fish your feet first.' In other words, don't try and throw your line as far as possible, the fish may be right at your feet. As the good book says, there is 'a time for every purpose under heaven.' When everyone else is trying too hard to do something obscure it could well be time to do the obvious.

Don't overlook the obvious

*It requires a very unusual mind to undertake
the analysis of the obvious.*
ALFRED NORTH WHITEHEAD

Bottled water and all-girl bands! Now why didn't you think of these?

The best solutions are often right in front of our eyes and we don't see them. As the Latin proverb says, 'Common sense is not very common.' We ignore things because they seem obvious. We see no room for creativity. When someone else has a great idea people often think: 'But that's obvious' or 'Why didn't I think of that?'

Think of all the ways the human body has been artistically portrayed and how many times the chair has been redesigned. From generation to generation, people continue to reinterpret 'the obvious'.

Why don't you try making the obvious more obvious?

Sportsmen well know the benefits of changing pace. In cricket or baseball a bowler or pitcher can completely bamboozle the person at bat by varying the pace of delivery. In tennis a player who can vary the speed of a serve or volley has the upper hand.

Change the pace

I took a speed-reading course and read War and Peace *in 20 minutes. It involves Russia.*

WOODY ALLEN

Some things move at just the right pace — like a burning cigar. Others could do with a little help: a faster snail would be less vulnerable.

Can your problem or idea be helped by a change in pace? Could it be made to last longer, like stockings and light bulbs? Or deteriorate sooner, like throwaway packaging? Microwaves have allowed us to have food cooked a lot faster and cameras have allowed us to capture flowers blooming and ourselves ageing.

Rush, speed, hasten, slow, delay, dawdle, linger, plod.

An audio tape played at twice the normal speed can make Pavarotti sound like 'The Chipmunks'. What would be the sound of a rock aging over 10 million years? Would it emit any sound at all?

> IT'S OUR SMALLEST AND FINEST MA'AM — THAT'S WHY IT COSTS MORE

Why do diamonds, the smallest of gems, cost so much? We can't eat them or find any practical domestic use for them. Why do we expect good things to come in small packages?

Explore paradox

Less is more.

LUDWIG MIES VAN DER ROHE

Nothing is something. Innovation is destruction. This sentence is false.

Paradoxes stimulate insight. They tap directly into our intuitive knowledge, just like poetry and music.

In essence, paradox contradicts logic and shows us how opposites are inextricably linked. Opposites exist by virtue of each other. We wouldn't have evil if there wasn't good. Up can't exist without down. In order to know light we must experience darkness. To understand positive we must know negative.

Knowing the relationship of opposites broadens our perspective and often leads to more creative solutions.

- What is a disorganised organisation?
- How can you create balance from confusion?
- How can you go back to the future?

> IT'S OUR NEW MINING MACHINE, WE CALL IT "FATHER MURPHY" - LIKE HIS SERMONS - VERY LONG AND BORING.

Many of us give our car a name: anything from 'Puddlejumper' to 'Doris'. In doing so we imbue them with characteristics that befit the name. If it's an old, slow but reliable car we'd probably use an old-fashioned but friendly sounding name, like that of an elderly aunt or uncle. What is our current problem? Will personifying it help? Is it a piece of machinery that we'd feel better disposed towards if it has a name? Will we forgive its foibles more easily if it has a personality we can relate to?

Personify

The piano has been drinking and the carpet needs a haircut.

TOM WAITS

Does the fruit chat when the lights go out? What do cars feel when put in the garage? Do trees weep when you cut them down? How does the wall feel being covered in plaster? Does your computer like its new upgrade?

Applying a persona to an object gets our creative juices flowing. A pen, a light bulb, a chair, a newspaper, a discarded idea — how would they think, feel and act if they were alive? Personify it. Become it. Give the problem human qualities. Ask these questions of your problem:

- What kind of person would it be?
- What would it love?
- Who gets on well with it?
- What clothes would it wear?
- What does it value?
- What is it good at?
- How does it feel about you?
- How does it greet others?
- What would it look like?
- What are its politics?
- What gender would it be?
- Can it act out of character?
- What are its strengths?
- What are its struggles?
- How does it walk?
- Does its attitude to people vary?
- What's its temperament? (Practical? Flirty? Macho? Kind? Bullying? Critical?)

Our lives only make sense to us looking backwards. We all have our dreams and anticipate our life story unfolding with a happy ending. We often see parallels to our own lives in books and movies. So when we face a problem we can ask how some other identity would handle it. Like a comic-book superhero, can our problem disappear into a phone booth and change identity from a mild-mannered Clark Kent into Superman?

Change identity

It is quite a three-pipe problem.

SIR ARTHUR CONAN DOYLE, 'THE RED-HEADED LEAGUE'

While personifying is making your problem or issue human, 'changing identity' is broader than this — it is making your problem into something else, whether animate or inanimate.

Consider what else the problem could be. If the problem was a song, how would it sound? Is it in tune? Loud? Soft? Melodious or screeching? What if it was a book, film, poem, CD, magazine, movie script, country or piece of clothing? Does it even have to be real? Could it become a myth or a dream?

Perhaps your problem has practical constraints. Are these constraints only real to you because of your own limitations?

T.S. Eliot's poem about our furry friends was elevated to cult status by Andrew Lloyd Webber's musical 'Cats'. After 'Benjamin Bunny' and 'Watership Down' rabbits became loved by urban children, even though they are noxious pests in the countryside. If we thought like an animal would we see our problems differently? How would a mouse like his trap designed?

Step into an animal's world

The Bluebird of Happiness long absent from his life, Ned is visited by the Chicken of Depression.

GARY LARSON

Walt Disney movie writers and cartoonist Gary Larson are experts at taking an animal's perspective. If you were designing a chair how would it be different if you were making it for an elephant? Or a mouse? Notice how this frees your mind of the restrictions it has when just designing for humans.

How would an animal look at your problem, product or service?

> IT'S HOT MUM, CAN I TAKE A COLD WATER BOTTLE TO BED?

On a very hot midsummer night, five-year-old Kim, a clever little boy of some imagination, came downstairs clutching a hot-water bottle. He asked his mother if she could fill it with iced water from the fridge. In his young head a cold-water bottle was just as logical as a hot one.

Think like a kid

Age 7 why
Age 17 why not
Age 37 because

DAVID CAMPBELL

There are numerous parallels between creative thinking and the thought patterns of playful children. A child's perspective puts us in a more curious state of mind.

How would a 10-year-old interpret your problem or issue? Looking to children for ideas and inventions has inspired whole new lines of research. Some companies invite kids in to talk to them and get their perspectives.

Play. Dress up. Laugh at what amuses you. Lie on the floor and draw moustaches on people in magazines.

It is not just imagining ourselves to be younger that can help us get ideas. Jump into the minds of people of all ages.

Owls have huge eyes for hunting in the dark. Some can see 50 times better than a human being. While an owl can't move its eyes to look to one side, it can turn its whole head around to look backwards.

Swap eyes

The real magic in discovery lies not in seeking new landscapes but in having new eyes.

MARCEL PROUST

Ever wondered what it would be like to have totally different visual powers? The fact is different living things literally see the world differently. We know, for example, that some animals such as dogs don't even see colours.

A frog's eye sees only certain things, such as the insects it wants to eat. A bee sees a flower as a runway upon which to land. Rabbits and fish have eyes positioned so they can see in front and behind them at the same time.

How does your problem look from a bird's perspective? An eagle not only has more visual acuity than us, it also tends to fly over its environment getting an overall perspective. A pet on the other hand often finds itself having to look up to its owner.

> HE HASN'T CHANGED HIS WARDROBE IN 20 YEARS — HE ALWAYS SAID BELL-BOTTOMS WOULD COME BACK!

What's hot, what's not, and why? What do you no longer buy? Read old magazines and check what's there and what is no longer in them. Some people just have a knack for knowing what's the new, new thing.

What's hot and what's not?

Fashion is made to become unfashionable.
COCO CHANEL

Look at the problem. Is it part of a pattern? Pattern-spotting requires us to look at the broader nature of things to find connections.

Trends are patterns. And trend recognition is one of the important skills for generating innovative ideas. What are people buying, reading, watching, eating, wearing? Don't neglect declining trends. For example, fewer face-to-face money transactions, less cigarette and fur coat sales.

There are trends in food, housing, music, hairstyles, magazine covers and habits to name just a few. What are some of the patterns of popular culture? Healthy fast food, environmentally friendly products, organics, alarm systems, catalogue shopping, sports clothes, gyms and warehouse bargain shopping. As people spend more time at work a growth industry is born for those who are able to do things for them at home. Cleaners, nannies, gardeners, pet-walkers, pet-groomers and personal trainers increase in demand.

Whenever there is a strong trend in one direction there is usually a 'revenge trend' in the other. Jennifer James, in 'Thinking In the Future Tense', calls this 'the dance of life'. It's like taking two steps forwards and one step back. The step back is like a hesitation but the overall trend is forwards. This can spur ideas and niche markets. For example, cigars became popular when smoking was outlawed in most establishments and the sale of meaty burgers went up when there was a boom in healthy eating.

'The uncreative mind can spot wrong answers, but it takes a creative mind to spot wrong questions.'
— Anthony Jay

Good questions create the best answers

Reason can answer questions, but imagination has to ask them.
RALPH GERARD

Questions are powerful assistants to creative thinking. In fact, asking questions is an art in itself. Questioning is part of a larger process of creativity. Questioning challenges our perception, excites our imaginations, kickstarts our thoughts into new directions and enables us to focus.

Speculate, ask why and why not. Pester the problem with Why? What? (And why?) Who? (And why?) Where? (And why?) When? (And why?) How much? (And why?) How many? (And why?)

Open-ended questions are also excellent for generating ideas because they allow for fresh, unanticipated answers to reveal themselves. These are the kinds of questions children are not afraid to ask. They may seem naïve at first but 'What if ... ?' questions encourage us to investigate options we might otherwise never explore.

> BOB THINKS HE WILL CATCH BIGGER FISH NOW HE HAS A BIGGER BOAT!

Just because we have a bigger boat doesn't mean we'll catch bigger fish. In corporate life investment in expensive new technology only gives us a competitive advantage until our competitors acquire the same equipment.

Do you really need a bigger boat?

You kids today have it easy. When I was a kid everything was HUGE. My dad was nearly four times bigger than me. You couldn't even see the tops of counters ... Then gradually everything became smaller until it was the manageable size it is today.

'BIZARRO' COMIC STRIP

Coming up with something new can easily involve rearranging what you've got. You don't always need a bigger boat.

Rearranging need not be something we just do every now and then with our living-room furniture. Often the answer is right there in front of our eyes. We just need to shift things around a little. By playing around with the pieces of a problem we can find a better fit.

Ask if it can be reorganised or rearranged. What other arrangement could be better? Will this improve it or create something else? How could offices, resources and staff be rearranged in your organisation to do a better job?

In his book 'The Tipping Point', Malcolm Gladwell explores the resurgence in popularity of Hush Puppies, 'the classic American brushed-suede shoes'. The comfortable middle-class shoe became trendy again when a few avant garde New Yorkers started wearing them. 'No one took out an advertisement ... Those kids simply wore the shoes when they went to clubs or cafés or walked down the streets of downtown ...'

Recycle

We seem to be going through a period of nostalgia, and everyone seems to think yesterday was better than today. I don't think it was, and I would advise you not to wait 10 years before admitting today was great. If you're hung up on nostalgia, pretend today is yesterday and just go out and have one hell of a time.

ART BUCHWALD

There comes a time for an idea and then there comes a second time.

You can generate new ideas by having a good all-round knowledge of old ones and recycling them in new and original ways.

Recycling ideas can work due to nostalgia, a discovery by a new generation or much better timing. Comebacks, however, don't just happen with fashions. Some patents for inventions in the past may now be more appropriate to develop today. And old science fiction books with futuristic ideas may not seem so crazy now.

Modern vending machines are a 'recycled' idea. The first vending machine was invented by Hero of Alexandria around 215 BC. When a coin was dropped into a slot, its weight would pull a cork out of a spigot and the machine would dispense a trickle of water.

Think about what you are throwing away. How long does your 'junk' stay outside your house when an inorganic refuse collection is due? Probably not long after the neighbours' kids have picked over it. You can make a lot of marmalade with waste orange peel after the juice has been extracted.

Waste not want not

The most remarkable thing about my mother is that for 30 years she served the family nothing but leftovers. The original meal has never been found.

CALVIN TRILLIN

Reconsider your rubbish. Many good ideas have been found in the bin. Designers and architects sometimes find that their best work is in their initial sketches or from what they literally fished out of the rubbish bin.

Every new idea creates by-products. Sometimes what you leave out can be as powerful as what remains. These leftovers are often seen as waste and discarded or ignored.

Look at what people throw out and what they keep. Wood shavings glued together make chipboard, plastic is made from petrol by-products and some facial treatments use fruit pips.

What 'waste' are you surrounded by? Hot air, paper, grumpy looks? Consider how you could use your leftovers to create something new.

If you don't know where to start, anywhere will do. Writer's block, the great curse of scribblers, can be cured by just writing something — anything — down. No matter how preposterous, putting your ideas on paper can open the floodgates of thought. Knowing what's obviously wrong can help us zero in on what's right.

Start with the ridiculous

*A little nonsense now and then,
is cherished by the wisest men.*

ROALD DAHL, 'CHARLIE AND THE CHOCOLATE FACTORY'

Silence, a blank page or a tense meeting can be uncomfortable and intimidating. To get ideas flowing, we need to just start with something, anything — even if it's crazy. Illogical, non-linear starts can be brilliant launch points.

Start with something wrong, ridiculous, misleading or inarticulate. Just start with something. Even start with a rubber chicken. Sounds silly, but the whole process of having ideas is often unclear, ambiguous and chaotic. There are no rules and there is no correct starting point.

The fastest way to shut up others around you is by saying or even subtly implying 'That was a bad idea.' While a ridiculous suggestion can be what sparks a great idea. Often people limit their creative thoughts for fear of what others might think. But when drumming up ideas, we need to call the whole notion of getting bad ideas into question. We often need 'dumb' ideas to spark our thinking and lift us to another level.

Don't hesitate to ask dumb questions and explore ridiculous proposals. You may stumble on a solution that's been overlooked.

Remember, who kicks the ball may not score the goal, but they may start a winning game. Be the angel's advocate. Try and keep ridiculous suggestions in the air and make them work.

COLUMBUS' LAST WORDS

In Columbus' time, Portuguese navigators were convinced the world was round; some had stood on cliff-tops and watched ships disappear gradually over the horizon. Philosophers and scientists since the time of Plato also believed it, but conventional wisdom and the vast majority of people, through biblical interpretation (e.g. 'He has fixed the earth firm, immoveable ...', 1 Chronicles 16:30) thought it was flat. Columbus ignored the common explanation, backed the judgement of his fellow navigators and sailed into history.

Examine the explanation

Travelling at over 30 mph will cause suffocation.
VICTORIAN ROAD RULE

Why do things happen? Fate, luck, hard work or punishment? Some explanations are more helpful, constructive and comforting than others. Explanations can determine our level of sympathy. They differ in the extent to which they attribute blame, elicit shame and motivate us to take action. By changing the nature of the explanation a person can get hugged rather than hit, put in hospital rather than jail or promoted rather than fired.

Explanations also come in and out of fashion, change over time, vary from group to group and culture to culture. Explanations are a huge, largely untapped source of creativity. Rare and even absurd explanations are often excellent catalysts for solving problems. For example, your boss finds you too intelligent and intimidating; that's why she 'forgets' to attend your meetings. Pick some big problems and re-explain them. Why do we fight? Why do we let others starve? Why do young people use drugs? Why do men die younger? Why don't women go bald?

Accepting explanations at face value can discourage us from suggesting something new. Just because a dominant explanation has survived unthreatened for decades it doesn't mean it's right. Challenge the orthodox explanations you use. Expect some flak and be aware that you may not sound as articulate as those holding more popular beliefs. Remember, there was a day when people believed the world was flat.

It is amazing how apparently lazy people can be transformed into energetic zealots when given tasks they enjoy. It's all a matter of perspective. People's brains and physiology work in different ways. Neuropsychologist Professor Howard Gardner says mankind is made up of at least seven basic types of intelligence: linguistic, mathematical, musical, spatial, kinaesthetic, interpersonal and intrapersonal. Think about a problem in the context of another's viewpoint.

Reframe

A weed is no more than a flower in disguise.

JAMES LOWELL

Remember there are numerous ways to frame a problem before thinking about how to solve it. Rewriting the problem in a new way changes its meaning so we can see it in a new light.

Sometimes words are loaded with pessimistic overtones, making the problem seem too hard to solve. Words can also prescribe blame, which inhibits getting others on board to work towards a solution.

When the problem's been unsolved for a long time, we probably need to reframe it.

For example:
- Are we hosting a discussion or facilitating a conflict?
- Is it an aggressive audience or unhappy guest?
- Is it resistance or discontent with the agenda?
- Were we making a noise or creating a disturbance?
- Was it a dysfunctional family or did some members just have a few quirks?
- Was the person reluctant or slow to warm?
- Are they being lazy or taking time out to gather energy?
- Did they lose their temper or find it?
- Are they survivors or victims?
- Is that a sweat or a natural glow?

> I SEE YOU HANDING OVER $20 BUCKS IN EXCHANGE FOR ME MAKING WILD GUESSES ABOUT YOUR FUTURE!

Michelangelo said, 'I saw the angel in the marble and carved until I set him free.' It's the silence between the musical notes, the space around the objects that can give us as much pleasure as the notes or the objects themselves. When a gypsy fortune-teller looks into a crystal ball what does she really see? Most likely it's our body language and non-verbal clues that she reads and feeds back to us.

Do a double take

Imagination is more important than knowledge.

ALBERT EINSTEIN

Stop for a minute and look hard at a familiar object. Refuse to accept its conventional identity. Allow yourself to look for a while. What else could it be?

Most of us have seen something that looks like something else; wood on a beach, a friend in a crowd, a person in the shadows.

These double-take moments are not limited to visual things. They can occur with words, sounds, smells and sensations. Was that an earthquake? Can you smell burning? Is that the phone? Did you just say what I think you did?

Seeing something for what it's not is what psychologists call contrary recognition. Rather than dismissing these instances as we normally do, we can explore these 'double take' moments to enhance our creativity. Noticing contrary identities to things can be a good way to get ideas and develop metaphors and analogies.

Manhole covers are round with slightly tapered edges or a small lip, because any other shape (apart from an equilateral triangle) could twist and fall down the hole.

Shape and form

A chair is a very difficult object. A skyscraper is almost easier. That is why Chippendale is famous.

LUDWIG MIES VAN DER ROHE

To the uneducated, an A is just three sticks.

EEYORE

We talk about the shape of things or how things are shaping up, but why are things the shape they are? What if the problem or idea were sleeker, chunkier or a completely different shape?

Comic-book hero Plastic Man could change shape in order to solve problems. Changing the shape of a familiar object can spark our thinking. Altering the shape of some foods means kids are more likely to eat them. Making TVs flat saves space. What if vases were square, TVs round, toasters hexagonal, kettles cubic, plugs triangular and telephones flat?

> IT'S NO GOOD TRYING TO HIDE DR. ROENTGEN — WE CAN SEE STRAIGHT THROUGH YOUR SILLY TRICKS!

In 1895 Wilhelm Conrad Roentgen was exploring the properties of cathode rays (i.e. electrons). He noticed a glowing fluorescent screen nearby and deduced it must have been fluorescing due to invisible rays from a partially evacuated glass Hittorf-Crookes tube he was using. Surprisingly the tube was surrounded in black paper, and the mysterious rays had penetrated the paper. Roentgen had accidentally discovered X-rays.

Savour your spilt milk

In every work of genius we recognise our own rejected thoughts.
RALPH WALDO EMERSON

Sometimes when grappling with one problem, we find a solution to another. Time and time again in the history of science, investigators have accidentally encountered phenomena that should not have occurred, recognised them as anomalies and revised their thinking to accommodate them. Remember, Alexander Graham Bell was working on designing a hearing aid when he invented the telephone.

Accidents can be important sources of information to generate new ideas — and not necessarily ideas related to what we are directly working on. An ability to use and notice accidental discoveries is a fundamental characteristic of entrepreneurs. If you're on the wrong track you could still be on the right track to something completely different. Means may become entirely detached from ends and become a worthwhile pursuit in their own right. In trying to find the right colour for our current project we may discover a new one. In checking meanings of words we may find totally different ones.

Learn to expect the unexpected. Serendipity is when we find things of value when we are not looking for them. We accidentally discover things that we weren't setting out to find. Be aware of these moments.

It is well accepted among educators that some students learn best with music in the background. Because the brain is programmed to pick up messages from words, music without lyrics is best. The Baroque music of Vivaldi, Pachelbel, Bach and Handel in particular, enhances learning and memory; their calming, soothing rhythms approximate the beating of the human heart.

Swing to the music

Music is a higher revelation than philosophy.
LUDWIG VAN BEETHOVEN

Music causes us to think eloquently.
RALPH WALDO EMERSON

Music can cause the controlling, analytical part of our minds to relax and our intuitive side to step in.

When was the last time you sat down and listened to some new music — ethnic drums, reggae, the sounds of nature, classical, jazz or rock 'n' roll?

Music has a powerful capacity to affect our mood. It can rekindle emotions that we usually leave untapped. It can be uplifting, thought-provoking, make us feel happy, hopeful, excited and energised, or sad and down in the dumps.

Sounds can also transport us. For example, bells can trigger us to recall places we have heard them: churches, weddings or funerals.

> IF EINSTEIN COULD EXPLAIN THE FUNDAMENTAL STRUCTURE OF THE UNIVERSE IN FIVE CHARACTERS — WHY DOES IT TAKE A 500 PAGE REPORT TO TELL US THE EDUCATION SYSTEM IS FAILING?

Have you ever noticed how truly wise and knowledgeable people are able to explain things in very simple terms, yet those with lesser skills are long-winded and pompous? Because they don't really understand what they are talking about, they tell you everything they think they know in the hope some of it will be right. One of the reasons Colin McCahon was a great painter was because of his ability to capture the simple essence of landscapes. Albert Einstein managed to describe the fundamental nature of the universe in five characters: $E=mc^2$.

Simplify

How difficult it is to be simple.

VINCENT VAN GOGH

Many fantastic ideas are so simple people often wonder what all the fuss was about. All factors being equal, simpler is better. Inside every good idea is a better one trying to get out. Creativity doesn't mean complexity. Many ideas are needlessly overcomplicated. People can get distracted by irrelevant details. Get rid of clutter.

Often we want clutter because we spent so long working on the problem that it's too dispiriting to abandon. We need to fight off the sentimental attachment we develop during our many hours of labour.

Simplicity is at a premium today as we have a tendency to overcomplicate things. In fact, as life becomes more complex and unfamiliar we yearn for simplicity. People go back to books, fountain pens and beachside baches as online magazines, computers and inner-city apartments boom.

Visuals need editing just like writing does. Things can be overcooked. Streamline, reduce, remove, trim, edit, delete, strip, eliminate. Repeatedly ask what's not necessary and what could be left out.

Everything you add to an idea can reduce the importance of the other elements. What you subtract can add to the importance of what's left. Remove a wheel, a leg or a wall. Sometimes by taking something away we add something. For example, 'low-fat', 'caffeine-free' and 'no deposit'.

There's a store in New York called 'Think Big'. There you can buy giant-sized versions of many products. It's amusing to see items of everyday use expanded to an unmanageable size. It makes us think about them in a totally different way. In 1949 'Popular Mechanics' magazine predicted that one day computers might weigh as little as one and a half tons!

Beef up or trim down

Life shrinks or expands in proportion to one's courage.

ANAÏS NIN

What caused 10 times more ice cream to be sold at Lionel's roadside dairy? Nicer food, better parking or a new children's play area? No, he simply painted a much bigger sign. Similarly, it was found that giving people trolleys rather than baskets in supermarkets makes them buy more. Simple shifts in size can make a difference.

We expect things to be certain sizes. Changing something's size can jolt our habitual thinking and surprise us.

How big is the problem or idea? Is bigger better? What if your problem or idea was as big as a rugby field or pinhead small?

Most people see things they value as larger. For example, they tend to think important people are taller than they are in person. What if you extended it, made it bigger, wider, higher, larger or longer? Why is your pen that length? Why is a computer mouse that size? Why aren't pills bigger? What if we all had larger offices?

Elephants are big and most birds are small. Is one, however, more important than the other? It is becoming more of a myth that size equals power and status. Smaller can also be just as good if not better. For example, doctors can now see inside us with tiny cameras, so they don't need to cut us open. And within the next 30 years, high-tech war machines could include tiny ant-sized robots that destroy tanks by crawling down their exhausts and wrecking their engines. Nanotechnology is a new field of science looking at how to make things smaller.

We tend to focus on what's urgent rather than on what's important. Our immediate problems may need to be fixed urgently, but the problems may still remain if we don't solve what's important. As the saying goes: 'When you're up to your arse in alligators, it's sometimes difficult to remember that your original objective was to drain the swamp.'

Be solution-focused

People want solutions not answers.

ANONYMOUS

The only difference between a problem and a solution is that people understand the solution.

CHARLES F. KETTERING

Most of us assume we need to understand the problem fully to solve it. In many cases, however, this leads us to get caught up exactly where others have been stuck before.

Few people are solution-focused. Discussions concerning problems dominate most meetings no matter what business we are in. If you are feeling frustrated in a meeting, have a look at how much time is spent on discussing problems. Ninety-nine percent of the time will probably be 'problem talk'. Sometimes the only solution that comes out of a meeting is 'Let's break for lunch.'

In addition, people become sceptical about change. This can produce an atmosphere of hopelessness that maintains the problem and limits creative solutions.

We need to remove fixed mental attitudes and narrowed thinking. One way to do this is to stop assuming that solutions will come from understanding the problem — especially when it comes to complex human problems or even wider social issues. Instead, ask what the goal is rather than what the problem is. This perspective can open up a multitude of options because it breaks free from the parameters imposed by the problem.

While no one still thinks straw can be spun into gold, there are parallels when fraudsters or con men of today claim to be able to build perpetual motion machines or sell stock in worthless companies with fictitious earnings. Greed often overcomes common sense. Then again, we shouldn't stop looking for elusive alchemies — highly efficient hydrogen-powered cars using water may be seen in the near future.

Explore myths, legends and fairytales

The universe is made of stories, not atoms.
MURIEL RUKEYSER

Vampires are make-believe, just like elves and gremlins and eskimos!
HOMER SIMPSON

In the fairytale of 'Rumpelstiltskin' an unscrupulous father told a king that his daughter could spin straw into gold in order that she might have a chance to marry the King's son. The hapless girl was locked in a castle tower to prove the claim. After a few nights of fruitless spinning the girl's desperate pleas for help were answered by a strange little man who magically appeared in her prison room. He claimed the girl's first-born in return for teaching her how to spin gold from the straw.

The girl married the prince but forgot her bargain until after the birth of her baby, when Rumpelstiltskin turned up to claim his fee. The distraught Princess begged him to reconsider and the little man took pity saying he would give up his claim to the child if the Princess could guess his name — he would return to hear her answer. The Princess sent her servants far and wide to search for clues. By chance one of her foresters came across the little man's house in the woods and discovered his secret.

When the little man returned the Princess finally told him his name was Rumpelstiltskin — enraged, he vanished, never to be seen again. Everyone except, presumably, the little man lived happily ever after.

> MY WATCH STOPPED AND I GOT SALVADOR DALI TO FIX IT.

How would Andy Warhol have interpreted your problem? What would Salvador Dali have done? If it was a song, how would Elvis have sung it? If it was played out as a movie, how would Marlon Brando have acted in it?

Tinker with style

Style means presenting an edited version of yourself to the world.
QUENTIN CRISP

The ultimate source of original ideas is you. Copying someone else is never the way to go. In developing your thinking, however, it doesn't hurt to consider how others you admire would have solved the problem or issue.

Reinterpreting is okay; hence, we talk of 'Lawrence Olivier's Hamlet'.

Art or architecture magazines are great sources of avant-garde design trends and reference to past trend makers. Similarly the art and design sections of quality bookshops contain compendiums of art, music and literary history.

If you're completely stuck for an idea, say on how Andy Warhol would handle a dinner party, go into an internet search engine and type in 'Warhol on food' — or maybe Mozart's clothes or Eminem's shoes, if you want to get a lead for fashion.

> IT'S BLUEBERRY JUICE WITH A STICK IN IT — WHEN REFRIGERATION GETS INVENTED I'LL CALL IT AN ICE BLOCK

Although liquids like fruit juice must have frozen solid during icy snaps in medieval times, no one thought of marketing them as Paddlepops or FruJus because there was no way of transporting or keeping them frozen outside the icy conditions they were created in. And who needed a frozen drink on a stick when it was 20 degrees below? If we are unconstrained by present technology and imagine anything is possible, will this enable our idea to become a reality?

Substance and structure

One only needs two tools in life: WD-40 to make things go, and duct tape to make them stop.

G.M. WEILACHER

If we make things from rubber we can stretch them; from glass they become clear and more fragile and from gold, more valuable. Water is used for many things in industry because it has an ability to change structure. Change your problem, product or issue to neon, plastic, gas, metal, fabric, paper, wicker or wood — does this stretch your thinking? How about if you ...

Heat it?	Soften it?	Harden it?	Strengthen it?	Weaken it?
Freeze it?	Fluff it?	Protect it?	Melt it?	Burn it?
Rot it?	Melt it?	Make it unbreakable, heavier or lighter?		

Another way to change substance and structure is to ask 'What if ...'
- Doors were concrete? (Vaults)
- Mattresses were filled with air or water? (Air beds/water beds)
- Tyres were solid rubber?
- Metal was light? (Aluminium or titanium)
- Houses weren't wood? (Igloos)
- Drinks were frozen? (Iceblocks)
- Soap wasn't solid? (Liquid soap)

> MY BOY, THE SECRET OF SUCCESS IN POLITICS IS SINCERITY — ONCE YOU CAN FAKE THAT — YOU'VE GOT IT MADE!

If you're making a substitute, make sure your substitute isn't counterfeit, that your claims are true. Remember you can fool some of the people some of the time and some of the people all of the time, but not all of the people all of the time.

Find a ring-in

The paperback is very interesting, but I find it will never replace the hardcover book — it makes a very poor doorstop.

ALFRED HITCHCOCK

What other solutions or procedures can you ring-in to solve your problem? What word can you change? What rules can be swapped? What materials? What approach? What ingredient? What part? How about substituting environments, emotions, body parts or procedures?

Some everyday substitutes include Blu-Tack, saccharin, gas, vitamins, paper bags, plastic money and titanium.

The recent war in Iraq has revealed the duplicity of Saddam Hussein and his use of doubles or look-alikes to deceive. It has also been revealed that Churchill may have used doubles during World War II. Now celebrities who fear kidnapping or who simply want to confuse the paparazzi are looking at employing doubles.

Interestingly, our sense of smell is an extraordinarily powerful stimulant for recall, falling off less rapidly than other sensory memories. It is one of the chemical senses, the other being taste. We appear to have an innate ability to detect bad smells — one-day-old babies can give facial expressions indicating aversion to nasty odours. Dogs and horses can smell fear in humans; work done by Austrian scientists indicates that a chemical secretion in sweat communicates the emotion, detectable by animals' sensitive olfactory receptors.

What's that smell?

Smell is a potent wizard that transports you across thousand of miles and all the years you have lived.

HELEN KELLER

What is the smell of a bad idea? Forget how the problem looks and switch the problem over to your other senses. How does it sound? If it was edible what would it taste like? What texture would it have? How would it feel in your hands? If it was a trip would it be bumpy? What about smell?

We know that most people are 'sensing' learners, relying on their five senses to explore and understand their worlds. Such sensing behaviour is instinctive. How often do we break down our experiential behaviour and ask what sense or senses we are using to deal with a problem? If we can isolate each sense, we can amplify or intensify our thoughts about a problem.

The 'Voyager 1' spacecraft, launched by NASA in 1977 contains a gold disc inscribed with 115 images, including symbols, maps, diagrams and anatomical charts, greetings in 55 languages and natural sounds of Earth such as birds and whales. The symbols and messages, inspired by the late Dr Carl Sagan, are diagrammatic and expressed in what is hopefully a universal code. The notion being, should an alien spacecraft manned by sentient beings of similar or more advanced knowledge than humans stumble across it, they will be able to decipher the inscriptions.

Symbolise

Condense some daily experience into a glowing symbol, and an audience is electrified.

RALPH WALDO EMERSON

Imagine if a spaceship filled with aliens landed and picked you as a spokesperson for Earth. How would you communicate? Symbols translate better than words. Symbols can say a lot quickly and they can speak cross-culturally and across languages. For example, the famous London underground map directs millions even though it is not representative. Symbolising something forces people to convert their problem into something that other people can immediately understand. It helps us to divine the essence of an issue. Translate your problem into a symbol. How would you express yourself, your company or your issues using symbols?

Symbols have strengths and weaknesses. For example, the international symbol for wool enhances the soft and elegant aspect of wool, while in other cases the presence of a symbol such as a brand mark can detract from the message or slogan.

Essentially, the criteria for a successful symbol is that it is: distinctive, simple, can be taken out of context and still be understood. The best symbols do more than just represent something. They also generate awareness of the beliefs and values behind the symbol.

Chinese characters, Egyptian hieroglyphs, road signs, medieval crests and sign language are excellent sources of symbols. What symbols do you conjure up when you think of the world, a person, loyalty, anger, happiness, sunshine, music, no smoking or danger?

Marechal Ferdinand Foch, the French soldier who became Supreme Commander of Allied Forces in World War I did not see aircraft as having any military value. After countless lives had been lost in pointless battles for useless territory and the war was won, Foch wrote of the war as having two phases: 'Attrition' and 'Decision'. Basically, his military strategy had deliberately entailed armies of foot-soldiers fighting each other to a standstill, wearing each other's resolve down until decisive action could be taken and the weaker enemy defeated. How many lives would have been saved if he had foreseen the potential of air power?

Hindsight and foresight

The future is here. It's just not widely distributed yet.

WILLIAM GIBSON

Step into a time machine with your problem or idea. Go back or go forwards in time. Be curious. How would people react? For example, many people thought frozen food and Saturday morning shopping would never take off, and when the first cinema opened in Hong Kong people initially had to be paid to go. The Chinese believed the people on the screen were evil 'moving spirits'.

Go into the past, before TVs, telephones, railways or roads. How would the problem be viewed historically? What if it existed then? What if it was solved back then? How would things be different now? Would the solution have succeeded better in the past?

People once thought radio would only be useful for Sunday sermons. And we know how, in 1949, IBM dismissed the idea of PCs because they thought world demand for computers would be satisfied with five mainframes. History is filled with examples of intelligent people failing to see the future potential of an idea.

Future vision is a skill. Most people close their minds to the future. Transporting your problem into the future creates a new context, new relationships, new perspectives and therefore new ideas.

There are many examples of product or brand names that have negative connotations when translated into other languages, causing offence or at best poor sales. When Chevrolet released the Nova in Mexico its poor sales confounded the company until someone pointed out that 'no va', roughly translated as a mix of Spanish and English, means 'no go'!

Translate

I desire the Poles carnally.

PRESIDENT JIMMY CARTER'S MISTRANSLATION IN A 1977 SPEECH IN POLAND

Teeth extracted by the latest Methodists.

ADVERTISEMENT FOR A HONG KONG DENTIST

What happens when you translate the problem or idea into another language? Or put the visual symbols into a different culture?

Translating your slogan or problem statement into another language and then translating it back again can get a whole new sentence format and stimulate ideas — and, if not, at least it's a bit of a laugh. There are computer programmes that can do this for you. However, when translation machines try to translate things, they often run into problems. One Japanese machine turned 'The Grapes of Wrath' into 'The Angry Raisins'. Another translated 'Out of Sight, Out of Mind' into 'The Invisible Idiot'.

"THANKS FLIGHT ATTENDANT— BUT ITS JUST A PROBLEM I'M TRAVELLING WITH!"

Einstein imagined himself riding on a beam of light. This helped him develop the theory of relativity. Travelling with a problem is a common method used by writers and scientists. Take the problem on an excursion. Just imagine yourself to be travelling with the thing you are pondering.

Hitch a ride

It is impossible to travel faster than the speed of light, and certainly not desirable, as one's hat keeps blowing off.

WOODY ALLEN

The process of travelling with the problem can create vastly new approaches that may otherwise elude. Travel in your mind with it. Do what it does; go where it goes. Become the rock at the bottom of a riverbed. Get inside a water or sewage system. Be the door that swings or gets slammed shut by the wind. Be the building that moves in the earthquake. Be the pollution. Go sit in the audience. Travel with sound waves through the air. Sit. Watch. Travel. Describe what happens. What do you see? Become one with it, get inside it, hitchhike, ride, swallow, inject, swim, fall, float and/or fly with the problem or issue.

Confronting the physical circumstances of a problem, in reality or mental imagery, is often called getting concrete. It often reveals practical difficulties or a new opportunity in a problem or idea.

Architects might visualise themselves in a house, the kitchen, walking on the deck, strolling into the garden, smelling the flowers and admiring the view. Computer programmers walk through the programmes and try to consider all possibilities. What if the game is played 100 times? Will people get sick of it?

Windsurfing began when someone attached a sail to a surfboard — the sport boomed. Now we have wakeboarding, parasailing and boogie-boarding, all derived from a similar root. A snowboard is a surfboard adapted for the mountains, similar experience, different medium.

Switch address

President Robbins was so well adjusted to his environment that sometimes you could not tell which was the environment and which was President Robbins.

RANDALL JARRELL, 'PICTURES FROM AN INSTITUTION'

Taking the problem out of its context helps us find novelty, changes how we see the issues and opens our minds to new connections. What other contexts could you put the idea in? Emotional, cultural, impoverished, stimulating, foreign, modern, vivid, historical or outer space? Moving your problem into fictional situations can free you from preconceptions and the restrictions of the current context. For example:
- A man stopped outside a hotel and immediately knew he was bankrupt. How? He was playing Monopoly.
- What do a sailboard, surfboard and snowboard have in common? Same object, different context.

Lewis Carroll's poem, 'Jabberwocky', gives us words that have no meaning yet conjure up images in our heads. We can visualise 'slithy toves gyring and gimbling in the wabe' but the images are fleeting — and if asked to describe a 'slithy tove' we feel we could tell what one looked like but just couldn't quite describe it. Some things defy description; they exist only in our imaginations but enable us to go to otherwise unimaginable places.

Visualise

The words of the language, as they are written or spoken, do not seem to play any role in my mechanism of thought. The physical entities which seem to serve as elements in thought are certain signs and more or less clear images which can be voluntarily reproduced and combined.

ALBERT EINSTEIN

Many highly creative people say they think in pictures not words. It's only later they try to verbalise their ideas. Often words force us down a linear path, whereas, in reality, thoughts are like language: full of contradictions, paradoxes, a bit of this, a bit of that, spiced with the tone and temper of the moment. Visual images encourage lateral thinking because they generate multiple meanings.

Another benefit of visualisation is it gets us out of our comfort zone. It allows us to take a new vantage point. Visualisation frees us from reality. It removes barriers, boundaries, fences, blocks and obstacles. We can fly, confront monsters, jump off cliffs and sing like rock stars.

> **OOH GLADYS! – IS THAT A NEW LAMPSHADE?**
>
> **NO. HAD IT FOR YEARS. IT'S THE ONE FRED WEARS ON HIS HEAD AT PARTIES**

There is a journalist's dictum, 'Dog bites man isn't news, man bites dog is.' Old wine barrels become plant pots, concrete blocks and planks become bookshelves. Wearing a lampshade on your head at a party has become such a cliché that it might be more unusual to see one on a lampstand.

Find other uses

If everyone is thinking alike then somebody isn't thinking.

GEORGE S. PATTON

Remember playing with magnets at school? Well, some design engineer certainly did. The world's fastest train, the Transrapid, travels between Berlin and Hamburg at 450 kph using magnetic levitation.

Unfortunately, more often than not we fail to see how things can be applied in a variety of situations. Numerous great ideas have been rejected because of our limited capacity to generalise and ask: 'What else could this be used for?' or 'How else could this be applied?'

If your solution fails in the original purpose you developed it for, remember to ask: 'What else could I do with this?'

Women's magazines collect tips about other uses for things. Put hairspray on dried flowers to keep them looking new. Use a shaver to remove fuzz off jerseys. Use baking soda on your teeth. Pour salt on spilt red wine. Use boots as flowerpots.

Oil is processed to make fuel for cars but it is also used to make medicines, explosives, pesticides, detergents, glues, polishes, plants, nylon, plastics and even make-up.

Clues for other uses are often seen in poorer countries. Leaves can be used as plates or carrying devices, wheelchairs are made from old bikes and toys are constructed from scrap metal. Look at what people throw out or try to sell — old exercise equipment, computers, etc. Is there any way these can be used alternatively? Maybe there is no such thing as a bad idea just a misplaced one.

The children's party game 'Pass it on' or 'Chinese whispers' where a simple message is whispered once to each person in a group, the larger the group the better, provides an example of how words can become jumbled and misheard, often with hilarious results. Because of different inflexions and multiple meanings of words, language can be a rich vein to mine in search of new ideas.

Wordplay

'Then you should say what you mean,' the March Hare went on. 'I do,' Alice hastily replied; 'at least — at least I mean what I say — that's the same thing, you know.'

LEWIS CARROLL, 'ALICE IN WONDERLAND'

How do you turn ordinary into extraordinary? Why do overlook and oversee mean opposite things? Isn't it strange how flammable and inflammable mean the same? Words tend to fix and define our thoughts and restrict our thinking. Words create subtle pressure for us to see a problem in a particular way.

Often the solutions to problems are in the words that describe them. We just need to play with them a little. Wordplay enables new and useful ideas to occur by breaking up linear logic. A great example of wordplay is Ernest Vincent Wright's 1939 novel 'Gadsby', it has 50,110 words, none of which contains the letter 'e'.

It is common for people, when they can't think of an idea, to write down a few words that describe the problem. They change the words around and associate them in new ways.

Change key words or try different pairs. Play with verbs and nouns. Make up anagrams. Transport words. For example, swap antonyms: How can you improve your creativity? How can you create your improvement?

Look at double meanings, figures of speech, similes, quotations, proverbs and puns. Play with words that sound like others, words that sound like sounds, words that can comically be confused for others and those that contradict each other.

When we zoom out details blur to become shapes or themes. Alfred Wegener stepped back and saw all the continents of the world like pieces in a jigsaw puzzle. He saw Africa's west coast fitted with the east coast of South America and theorised that they were all part of a whole. Hence the theory of continental drift arose.

Zoom in or fade out

*Where the telescope ends, the microscope begins.
Which of the two has the grander view?*

VICTOR HUGO

Imagine working on a huge jigsaw. To do so you would need to work in small sections — the trees, the edges, the people and sky — while always keeping the big picture in mind. Most people, however, get locked into small details and forget to step back to gain a wider perspective.

Literally zooming in and away from the problem can make it possible to generate new perspectives. We can mentally stop at each level to find the best viewing platform from which to step out and gather ideas. Seeing the problem from different levels can require different problem-solving methods.

Say our problem is a blocked road with traffic congestion. We can see this from a number of different levels. First, we have the person in a car in a traffic jam. Then a line of cars. Then the whole traffic jam. Then we can move onto the entire road network. Then the overall design of the city. Then the whole country's road designs. And then the whole world's road systems become involved. Here you move from the more specific to the more general. From bits to clusters to a whole. Like using rungs in a ladder you can move up or down depending on whether you want to look at the problem closer or further away. Take a glimpse from a distance. Walk or fly around it or stand right next to it. Film directors do this.

APOLOGIES TO LEONARDO

It is no coincidence that some of the great deals and alliances of history have been sealed over the dining table. Some of the central symbolism of the Christian Church was derived from a supper. We get to know and understand people through sharing meals with them. On an everyday level, wedding breakfasts are celebrations of union, and guests in commerce or government the world over are fêted at banquets.

Break bread

If Jesus Christ were to come today, people wouldn't even crucify him. They would ask him to dinner, and hear what he had to say ...
THOMAS CARLYLE QUOTED IN D. A. WILSON, 'CARLYLE AT HIS ZENITH'

Sharing a meal with friends, colleagues, or even strangers, can be the most pleasant and rewarding of human interactions. There are layers of meaning in communal eating that parallel the world of ideas.

Preparation of food is a creative act in itself, and 'mealtime' has overtones of generosity, conviviality, celebration, friendship, communication and sharing, not to mention sustenance, nurturing and energy.

It matters little if food is shared at a restaurant or in a private home, indoors or out. The meal table is neutral territory where manners and hospitality are paramount.

It is under these circumstances that nascent ideas can take shape, particularly if lubricated with some juice of the grape or grain! If you want others' inputs to help solve a problem, book a restaurant table or put on a meal with friends and colleagues. Set out the problem for them then let conversation flow. It may take half an hour to relax and feel comfortable, then the next hour or so is probably the most productive. Someone will make a suggestion and another will add to it and so on until it takes tangible form. Take notes. Remember though, after a couple of hours you will have covered most of what can be usefully achieved. Beyond that things are apt to get silly if too many bottles appear.

A writer of our acquaintance, who is also a martial arts instructor, swears that his rigorous workout regime enhances his creativity and that he does his best work in his post-exercise periods. Another businessman told us he got the inspiration for his coffee business while he was out running.

Exercise

I can feel the wind go by when I run. It feels good. It feels fast.

EVELYN ASHFORD

'Use it or lose it' is a truism to be heeded. If you are stuck for an idea, or feeling stale, take some exercise. Go for a run or a walk. Go to the gym, ride a bike, it doesn't matter. Not only will your body feel better and thank you for it, you may well have a new insight while you are out and about. You are likely to think far more clearly when you are feeling refreshed and revived.

Ensuring you have a healthy mind in a healthy body isn't just an old wives' tale, there is a strong body of scientific evidence to support the notion. Exercise stimulates the metabolism and lifts energy levels. As Ralph Waldo Emerson said: 'Intellectual tasting of life will not supersede muscular activity.'

While there are myriad fitness and creativity programmes available it's important to remember exercise doesn't just promote energy but also the sense of rhythm and balance that exercise can bring.

If you feel good walking early in the morning, with the sun warming your back, there is a perfectly sound physiological reason for it. In 1958 an American scientist discovered the hormone serotonin is produced by the pineal gland. The pineal gland functions as the body's internal biological clock, telling us, among other things, when it is time to wake, sleep, and how to adapt to seasonal changes. Serotonin promotes emotional warmth, calmness and inner peace. When the correct amount of serotonin is present in the brain, it is thought that people can 'think straight'.

> I THINK YOU'RE SEARCHING THE WRONG WEB!

If nothing else comes to mind, type in your own name and see how many others in the world have the same moniker. Maybe email them and see how they would tackle your problem. You may get short shrift, or you may get an interesting insight.

Search the web

The Internet is so big, so powerful and pointless that for some people it is a complete substitute for life.

ANDREW BROWN

A computer terminal is not some clunky old television with a typewriter in front of it. It is an interface where the mind and body can connect with the universe and move bits of it about.

DOUGLAS ADAMS, 'MOSTLY HARMLESS'

If you are at your lowest ebb ... search the web! While it is an obvious and common solution to search the web, it doesn't make it a bad place to start. The web is full of surprises and therefore a fantastic resource to kickstart your creativity.

Try searching for the obvious, the abstract or the opposite of what you are looking for. Why not type in a feeling like 'happiness' as opposed to a solid noun like 'bed'? Or try the opposite — for example, if you want to find out more about goodness look up evil (akin to slapping an encyclopaedia on your genitals, according to one search result). Look up 'fat' and you will find it is a bigger killer than Aids or terrorism. All this leads to new doors opening to novel pathways of thought, which is exactly what you need to stimulate fresh ideas.

Rehashing the words of popular songs is one of the easiest ways to parody a topic. It's a common trick of comedians and easily understandable by an audience familiar with a tune. Music is also a wonderful accelerant for a message; the poetry in song lyrics often sounds banal or nonsensical without the melody.

Explore parody

The secret to creativity is knowing how to hide your sources.

ALBERT EINSTEIN

Parody changes perspectives and therefore opens up our imaginations. Parody presupposes knowledge over the original thing you are parodying and hence flatters people's intelligence when they recognise the original source.

Using famous speeches, songs or nursery rhymes is a common form of humour and can revive a well-worn topic. Shakespeare's Julius Caesar has had a fair share of parodies written around it:

'Friends, Romans, countrymen, lend me your ears.'
'What have you got in that sack?'
'Ears.'

Ask how the concept of parody could help your idea. How about changing the lyrics of a popular song? For example, 'I might come home Bill Bailey' or 'I'll shake your nerves and I'll rattle your brain'.

'Uncle Sam Needs You' posters from World War I have become an icon of design, adapted and modified down the years for all kinds of different causes. Rubber masks of political figures and celebrities abound. Is there a political figure or issue that has relevance to your problem that could be twisted to suit?

Pull from politics and protest

The Gulf War — waged from bombers high above the fray and reported by carefully controlled journalists — made war fashionable again ... It almost made war fun.

CHRIS HEDGES, 'WAR IS A FORCE THAT GIVES US MEANING'

Politics and protest are commonly drawn on in order to sell ideas. Clothing has taken on a military look. Protection gear may become the new black.

What political or social message does your problem have, or does it need one? Or use political concepts or sound bites to generate new ideas. For example, how could you use 'We're smoking them out' (George W. Bush) to help with your anti-smoking campaign?

Peace is a hot concept right now. How could the concept of peace help with your problem? Could having a Ba'ath party help sell your aromatherapy? Could a woman wearing a burka help promote your weight-loss programme?

The intuitive mind 'invents' while dreaming. Many well-known writers and scientists have been able to conceive ideas during sleep. Physicist Niels Bohr visualised atomic structure when dreaming about the orbits of planets around the sun. Thomas Edison kept a pencil and paper by his bed and would write down ideas that came to him in the night. Robert Louis Stevenson was able to dream entire narratives and change them in another dream if he was unsatisfied.

Sleep on it

*We are such stuff
As dreams are made on, and our little life
Is rounded with a sleep.*

WILLIAM SHAKESPEARE, 'THE TEMPEST'

It's a paradox of creativity that sometimes when we stop thinking about a problem we come up with an answer. A common example occurs when we meet an acquaintance whose name has temporarily slipped our mind. Our brain goes into overdrive, desperately running through a list of names — yet we get no closer, only more confused. If we forget about it for a while — BINGO! The right name appears in our heads as if by magic.

Similarly, sleeping on a problem can crack it for us. Instead of worrying it to death, we should allow ourselves to go to bed with the problem in the back of our mind. During sleep the subconscious takes over and sifts through the problem and its component parts for us. Remarkably, we will often wake to find we can see the answer to our previously insoluble problem with rare clarity.

Keep a pad by the bed for just such an eventuality. Scribble down the thoughts you have if you wake in the night. (Catch Your Thoughts, page 55.) Your dreams, which shouldn't be interpreted too literally, can nevertheless provide strong metaphorical insights.

Bibliography

Adams, James. *Conceptual Blockbusting*. Stein & Day, 1976.

Bennis, Warren. *Organising Genius*. Addison/Wesley, 1997.

Calvin, William H. *How Brains Think*. Basic Books, 1996.

Czikszentmihalyi, Mihaly. *Creativity. Flow and the Psychology of Discovery and Invention*. HarperCollins, 1996.

Emmerling, John. *It Only Takes One*. Simon & Schuster, 1992.

Fisher, Marsh. *The Idea Fisher: How to Land that 'Big Idea' and Other Secrets of Business Creativity*. Peterson's/Pacesetter Books, Princeton, NJ, 1995.

Fritz, Robert. *Creating*. Fawcett Colombine, NY, 1991.

Gardner, Howard. *Multiple Intelligences: The Theory and Practice*. Basic Books, 1993.

Gladwell, Malcolm. *The Tipping Point*. Little Brown & Company, 2000.

Goodman, Joel. *Laffirmations: 1001 Ways to Add Humor to Your Life and Work*. Health Communications, 1995.

Harman, Willis & Rheingold, Howard. *Higher Creativity*. JP Tarcher, 1984.

Hutcheson, Mike. *#1 Best Seller*. Hazard Press, 2000.

LeBoeuf, Michael. *Imagineering*. Berkley Publishing Group, 1986.

Lehmkuhl, Dorothy & Cotter Lamping, Dolores. *Organising for the Creative Person: Right Brained Styles for Conquering Clutter, Mastering Time and Reaching Your Goals*. Crown Publishing, NY, 1993.

McKay, Charles. *Extraordinary Popular Delusions and the Madness of Crowds*. Crown Publishing, reprint edition, 1995.

McMurphy, John H. *Secrets from Great Minds*. Amaranth Publishing, Dallas, TX, 1995.

Moore, Pete. *E=mc². The Great Ideas That Shaped Our World*. Quintet Publishing, 2002.

Schank, Roger. *The Creative Attitude: Learning to Ask and Answer the Right Questions*. Macmillan, NY, 1988.

Schick, Theodore & Vaughn, Lewis. *How to Think About Weird Things*. Mayfield Publishing, 1999.

Wycoff, Joyce & Richardson, Tim. *Transformation Thinking: Tools and Techniques That Open the Door to Powerful New Thinking for Every Member of Your Organization*. Berkley Publishing Group, 1995.

Further reading

Czikszentmihalyi, Mihaly. *Flow: The Psychology of Happiness*. Rider, 1992.

Higgins, James M. *101 Creative Problem Solving Techniques: The Handbook of New Ideas for Business*. New Management Publishing, NY, 1994.

Koestler, Arthur. *The Act of Creation*. Pan Books, London, 1966.

Michalko, Michael. *Thinkertoys*. Ten Speed Press, Berkeley, CA, 1991.

Osborn, Alex F. *Applied Imagination*, third edition. Charles Scribers Sons, NY, 1963.

Pinker, Stephen. *How the Mind Works*. Penguin, 1997.

Spelling, Aaron. *A Prime Time Life: An Autobiography*. St. Martin's Press, 1996.

Von Oech, Roger. *A Kick in the Seat of the Pants*. Harper & Row, NY, 1986.

Von Oech, Roger. *A Whack in the Side of the Head*. Warner Books, 1988.

Westcott, Malcolm. *Toward a Contemporary Psychology of Intuition*. R & W Holt, 1968.

Articles

Boring, E.G. 'A History of Introspection', *Psychological Bulletin* 50, 1953, pp. 169–189.
Kiechell II, Walter. 'The Politics of Innovation', *Fortune*, April 1988, pp. 131–132.
Rosenfeld, Anne H. 'Music, the Beautiful Disturber', *Psychology Today*, Dec. 1985, pp. 48–56.
Swasy, Alecia. 'Kimberly-Clark Bets, Wins on Innovation', *Wall Street Journal*, 27 Nov. 1991.
Young, John G. 'What Is Creativity?', *Journal of Creative Behaviour.* 2nd Quarter, 1985, pp. 77–87.

Rebecca Webster can be contacted at welpa@xtra.co.nz
Mike Hutcheson can be contacted at hutch@lighthouseideas.com